j973
HOO

Hoobler, Dorothy.

The Jewish American
family album.

$19.95   07/30/1997

DATE			

THE JEWISH AMERICAN
FAMILY
ALBUM

THE JEWISH AMERICAN
FAMILY
ALBUM

DOROTHY AND THOMAS HOOBLER
Introduction by Mandy Patinkin

OXFORD UNIVERSITY PRESS • NEW YORK • OXFORD

Authors' Note

There are several systems for transliterating Hebrew words into the Roman alphabet. For example, the name for the midwinter Feast of Dedication may be written as *Hanukkah* or *Chanukah*. The editors of this book have generally used the spellings found in *Webster's Ninth New Collegiate Dictionary*. However, where the quotations cited in this book used different spellings, we have retained them.

Oxford University Press

Oxford New York
Athens Auckland Bangkok Bombay
Calcutta Cape Town Dar es Salaam Delhi
Florence Hong Kong Istanbul Karachi
Kuala Lumpur Madras Madrid Melbourne
Mexico City Nairobi Paris Singapore
Taipei Tokyo Toronto

and associated companies in
Berlin Ibadan

Design: Sandy Kaufman
Layout: Greg Wozney
Consultant: Riv-Ellen Prell, associate professor of American Studies, University of Minnesota

Published by Oxford University Press, Inc.,
200 Madison Avenue, New York, New York 10016

Oxford is a registered trademark of Oxford University Press

Library of Congress Cataloging-in-Publication Data

Hoobler, Dorothy.
The Jewish American family album / Dorothy and Thomas Hoobler.
p. cm. — (American family albums)
Includes bibliographical references and index.
1. Jewish families—United States—History—Juvenile literature.
2. Jews—United States—History—Juvenile literature.
[1. Jews—United States—History.]
I. Hoobler, Thomas. II. Title. III. Series.
E184.J5H655   1995
973'.04924'00922—dc20

94-43460
CIP
AC

ISBN 0-19-508135-8 (lib. ed.); ISBN 0-19-509935-4 (trade ed.); ISBN 0-19-509125-6 (series, lib. ed.)

9 8 7 6 5 4 3 2

Printed in the United States of America
on acid-free paper

Cover: The Freiberg family in Cincinnati around 1903.

Frontispiece: The Blacher family in Rhode Island around 1905. They immigrated from Poland.

Contents page: Howard Nevelow lights the Hanukkah candles at Agudas Achim synagogue in San Antonio, Texas, 1937.

CONTENTS

INTRODUCTION
by Mandy Patinkin

y story as an American Jew begins with my Grandpa Max, who was born to poor parents in a shtetl in Poland in about 1888. His father was a "Yeshivah bocher," a learned man in Jewish scriptures, who made a meager living as a teacher. Max's mother ran a small candy and vegetable shop to supplement the family income. At age 11 Max quit school and became an apprentice in a leather shop. But in 1905, when the czar's army came to the village to impress the young men for military service in Siberia during the Russo-Japanese War, Max put a pack on his back and crossed the German border to book passage to America.

Like many others who arrived at Ellis Island, Max was met by the Hebrew Immigrant Aid Society, which helped him find lodging and a job in New York City. He later joined relatives in Chicago, where he worked packing cigar boxes and as an usher at the Palace Theater.

Max earned enough at the cigar factory to help bring another brother to Chicago, but a guarantee of a job was then necessary to come to America. Max asked his boss to supply the job, but the boss angrily turned him down. That night Max Patinkin decided to go into business for himself. He invested his savings in a horse and wagon and became a junk peddler.

Grandpa Max became the family patriarch and devoted himself to philanthropic causes, notably on the board of the Hebrew Immigrant Aid Society—coming full circle.

The business prospered and expanded, and by the time I entered the picture People's Iron & Metal Company was an important part of the recycling business and employed many relatives, including my father. I was named after my Grandpa Max, whose Hebrew/Yiddish name was Menachem Mendel.

My mother's grandparents came from the town of Skud, Latvia, and were assigned the name Scudder when they arrived at Ellis Island. My great-grandfather was a learned man, a rabbi, chazzan (cantor), mohel (who performs ritual circumcision), and schochet (ritual slaughterer). They ended up in Davenport, Iowa—which needed one person to provide all those services for the Jewish community. Later, Morris worked at Swift & Co. in Chicago, supervising its kosher butchering operation.

When I grew up on the South Side of Chicago, our whole world revolved around the synagogue. My parents were members of the Men's Club and the Sisterhood. I went to Hebrew school five days a week, as well as on Sunday; on Saturday I was in the boys' choir. And I went to a Hebrew-speaking camp for two years. I was a rebel and wouldn't study, but I made a deal: I got myself cast as Tevye in the all-Hebrew camp production of

Fiddler on the Roof—and that was my Hebrew work for the summer.

Today I have two boys of my own and a wonderful wife, and my Jewishness informs my entire life. I do the rituals and the holidays, and I love my Jewishness. I love the tradition. The religious part of it is something very personal to me. It's something I define and have made up for myself. But the traditional aspects of belonging to a history of people are what I love the most—the comfort that I feel through the ancestral links of centuries, especially that of my own father, my grandfather, and what their lives were about.

Early in my career, people would say to me, "You're a Jewish actor." I took offense because I wanted to play everything. And indeed, the theater never typecast me as a Jew. I was Che Guevara, I was Georges Seurat, I was anybody. I was never Jewish. And yet, it took me quite a while, and maybe the birth of my own sons, and maybe my marriage, and maybe experiencing the anti-Semitism that I denied as a boy, to make me finally realize that everybody I play is Jewish. It is how I look at the world.

When I was a boy I went to temple every Shabbos, and every Friday night. There I got the message that we're generous people, that we're benevolent people, that we're caretaking people, that we're good people. There's a word in Judaism, *tzedakah,* which means to give charity. And the phrase

Tikkun olom, to repair the world. I love those words, and I rejoice when my children put them into action by doing things like giving their money or their time to charitable causes they've chosen.

Our children are going to have a very different experience than either of us had. For my wife, who grew up in Los Angeles, her Jewishness, her Jewish understanding, was social activism. My Jewish understanding was the synagogue. We have tried to bring up our children as Jews by teaching them at home, through experiences of traditional religious holidays.

We have made our own Haggadah for Passover. We make our own prayers that are a combination of our prayer book, of Jewish prayers that we know, of Shakespeare, of e. e. cummings, of all kinds of people—anything I hear that I believe in, that echoes the ideas that I felt that Grandpa Max embodied. The generosity, the caretaking, contributing beyond just our own community.

I love Yiddish songs because they tell stories—and they're almost all stories about the journey of Jewish families. In 1993 President Clinton asked me to sing for the dedication of the Holocaust Museum at the White House. The audience included not only the presidents of countries all over the world but Holocaust survivors. The last song I sang was in Yiddish, and it was "Yossel, Yossel." And an old man came up to me, and he said, "Young man, I was liberated from Auschwitz, and if 40 years ago someone had come up to me and said, '40 years from today, you will be standing at the White House and an American Jewish boy will be singing "Yossel, Yossel,"' I never would have believed it." It was a great moment.

Another of my favorite Hebrew words is *rachmones,* which means compassion. That's what we try to teach our children—compassion for each other, for our family, and for the world.

Patinkin as Iñigo Montoya in The Princess Bride.

Mandy Patinkin and Kathryn Grody with their two sons, Isaac (left) and Gideon Grody-Patinkin in 1990.

Mandy Patinkin is an *actor and singer who has appeared on Broadway, in numerous films, and starred in the CBS television drama "Chicago Hope." He won a Tony Award for his role as Che Guevara in the 1980 production of* Evita *and was nominated for a Tony for his 1984 role in* Sunday in the Park with George. *His movie credits include* The Princess Bride, Yentl, *and* The Music of Chance. *His first solo album was released in 1989; on his most recent release,* Mandy Patinkin: Experiment, *he sings popular American classics. Patinkin and his wife, writer/actress Kathryn Grody, live in New York with their two sons, Isaac and Gideon.*

The Patinkin family meets for a family reunion every three to six years. Here, in Hanover, Illinois in 1983, Mandy Patinkin is seated on the ground at right, holding his son Isaac. Standing directly behind him is his wife, Kathryn. His mother, Doris Patinkin Rubin, is seated at the right end of the second row; his sister, Marsha, is standing in the back row, eighth from left. The children in the front row hold portraits of Max and Celia Patinkin and of Mandy's father (right).

At this 1935 Patinkin family reunion in Chicago, Max Patinkin (second row, center) is seated next to his wife, Celia. Their four children are in front: Lillian (far left, holding baby); on the floor, Lester (Mandy's father) and Harold (known as Uncle Schmully), holding their grandparents' portraits, and Ida.

CHAPTER ONE

THE PEOPLE OF THE BOOK

The story of the Jewish people begins more than 3,500 years ago. It is retold in the Bible, the Jewish holy book that is called Tanak in Hebrew. Abram (or Abraham) was a shepherd who lived in Ur, part of Mesopotamia (the "land between the rivers"—today's Iraq). Seeking better pasturelands, Abram with his wife, Sarah, led a group of other herdsmen south. Because Abram spoke Hebrew, a Semitic language, his people were called Hebrews.

According to Genesis, the first book of the Bible, God appeared to Abram and promised to make his descendants a great nation that would live in Canaan—the Promised Land. "Now the Lord said unto Abram, 'Get thee out of thy country, and from thy kindred, and from thy father's house, unto the land that I will show thee. And I will make of thee a great nation, and I will bless thee, and make thy name great; and be thou a blessing" (Genesis 12: 1–2).

Abram and his family settled in Canaan, the land that God had promised, in present-day Israel. He, his son Isaac, and his grandson Jacob are known as the patriarchs, or fathers, of the Jewish people.

According to the Bible, one night Jacob met a stranger and wrestled with him in the darkness. His opponent revealed himself as an angel of God and gave Jacob the name Israel, which means "he who strives with God." Jacob's twelve sons became the ancestors of the Twelve Tribes, or families, of Israel. Thus the Jews were called Israelites.

But then famine came to the land of Canaan. Jacob's son Joseph, who had earlier been sold as a slave by his jealous brothers, by now had become the chief adviser to the pharaoh, or ruler of Egypt. He invited his father and his brothers and their families to come to Egypt to find relief.

Later a new pharaoh came to power in Egypt and enslaved the Hebrews. God appeared to Moses, who had been adopted by the pharaoh's daughter as an infant, and told him to lead the Hebrews out of Egypt. Moses asked what he should say if the Hebrews asked who commanded him to do this. God replied, "Tell them The God Who Is sent you." In Hebrew, this name was Yahweh; devout Jews regard it as so sacred that they neither write nor pronounce it, substituting words that mean "the Lord" or "the Name."

When the pharaoh refused to set the Hebrews free, God told Moses to instruct his people to kill a lamb or a young goat and smear its blood on the doorways of their houses. Then God went through Egypt, killing the first-born in every house except those of the Hebrews. He "passed over" the houses with blood on the doorways. Passover is a Jewish celebration to commemorate this event.

This punishment frightened the pharaoh, and he allowed Moses to lead the Hebrews out of Egypt. The departure from Egypt is called the Exodus, a sacred event in Jewish history. Most historians date it around 1250 B.C.E. (before the common era). After crossing the Red Sea, the Hebrews entered the Sinai Desert. Moses went to Mount Sinai, where God gave him laws, or commandments, for people to follow. These Ten Commandments have become the ethical standard for Western civilization—forbidding, among other things, murder, theft, lying, and adultery. God's command that "Thou shalt have no other gods before Me" formed the basis of monotheism, or the belief in one God, which later became part of Christianity and Islam.

For 40 years, the Hebrews wandered through the Sinai Desert. At last they entered the land of Canaan and conquered its inhabitants. They built an Ark of the Covenant—a chest of acacia wood and gold that contained the tablets on which the commandments were inscribed. Its name refers to the covenant, or agreement, that God made with Moses in the desert: if the Hebrews worshiped God as the one God and followed his commands, he would make them his chosen people and give them possession of the land of Canaan. Worship of Yahweh was led by a high priest and lesser priests, all of whom belonged to the tribe of Levi (one of Jacob's 12 sons).

Around 1025 B.C.E., when the 12 tribes faced a threat from the neighboring Philistines, the Hebrews united into the kingdom of Israel. Under David, their greatest king, the Hebrews conquered the land that stretched from Mesopotamia to Egypt. When David captured Jerusalem, he made it the political and religious capital of Israel.

King Solomon, David's son, built a Temple in Jerusalem. The priests at the Temple began to copy and preserve the sacred texts that form part of the Bible.

After Solomon's death, Israel split into two kingdoms: Israel in the north and Judaea in the south. The southern kingdom was named for the tribe of Judah; from this word came the name Jews.

The period of the two Israelite kingdoms was a time when great prophets appeared. A prophet was a person who was believed to receive messages from God. Prophets such as Amos, Isaiah, and Jeremiah criticized the injustices—such as neglect of the poor—that they saw in the two kingdoms as well as lapses in the worship of God. Amos predicted that God would al-

In 1922, students and teachers at the Israelitsche Volksschule (Jewish School) in Essen, Germany, plant a vegetable garden.

low the Assyrians to conquer Israel because of the injustice of its people. The prophets brought into Judaism a concern with social justice.

In 721 B.C.E., Israel was conquered by the Assyrians, who exiled its people. The 10 tribes who had lived there ceased to practice their religion and disappeared from history. The kingdom of Judaea survived until 586 B.C.E., when the Babylonians captured Jerusalem and destroyed the Temple. Afterward, the Judeans, or Jews, were sent to Babylon. During this Babylonian Exile, the Jewish com-

munity remained faithful to their God. They gathered in meeting places to pray together and study the Scriptures.

Ezekiel, a prophet who lived among the Babylonian exiles, declared that God had allowed this period of suffering to prepare the Jewish people for new greatness and holiness. Ezekiel also declared that God would punish or reward each person for his or her actions, rather than punish or reward the people as a group. The idea of personal responsibility for one's actions and the requirement to do good works have become central features of Judaism.

Cyrus of Persia conquered the Babylonians in 538 B.C.E. and allowed the Jews to return to Jerusalem. Many chose to do so. The Second Temple was built by the year 516, and the priests resumed the traditional ceremonies.

Some Jews stayed in Babylon while remaining steadfast to their faith. This was the beginning of the Diaspora, or dispersion of the Jews to communities outside Israel. However, they still looked to Jerusalem as the center of their faith.

Around 450 B.C.E., a scholar from Babylon named Ezra went to Jerusalem and called Jews to hear a reading of the law of Moses. Many scholars believe that this was the version of the Torah (which means "teaching" or "law") that exists today. The Torah is the most important part of the Hebrew Bible.

It consists of the first five books, from Genesis to Deuteronomy, and contains the story of creation as well as the history of the Jews from Abraham to Moses. According to tradition, God dictated the Torah to Moses at Mount Sinai.

The Torah contains many laws besides the Ten Commandments, as well as instructions for rituals and other religious practices. The Torah lists the basic dietary laws, or kashruth, that observant Jews follow; these laws originated because certain foods were considered unclean. Kosher ("fit" or "proper") meat comes from animals with cloven hooves that chew their cud—cattle and sheep; pork, the meat of pigs, is forbidden. Any food taken from the sea has to have gills and scales; shrimp and shellfish are forbidden. Milk and milk products may not be consumed with meat and meat products at the same meal. The rules of butchering meat were also set forth in the Torah.

Setting down a permanent version of the Torah in writing had important consequences for Jewish life. Though the priests of the Temple still carried out ceremonies, every Jew could learn to read and study the Torah. Respect for education thus became a traditional Jewish value. Some Jews call themselves "the people of the Book," signifying their devotion to the laws of the Torah.

Around 330 B.C.E. Alexander the Great conquered the Persian Empire, which included the Jewish people in Judaea. After Alexander's death, his generals divided up his conquests. Judaea fell under the control of the Seleucid dynasty, which was Greek. A later Seleucid ruler, Antiochus IV, stole some treasures from the Temple, and in

Jewish children on a street in Zabludow, Poland, in 1916. From about 1600 to the time of the Holocaust, more Jews lived in Poland than in any other nation in the world.

165 B.C.E., Judas Maccabeus ("the hammerer") and his brothers raised a revolt against him. After their victory, Maccabeus's family, the Hasmoneans, rededicated the Temple in a ceremony celebrated today in the Jewish feast of Hanukkah.

The Hasmoneans established a new kingdom of Israel, which lasted for about a century. In 63 B.C.E., Judaea was absorbed into the Roman Empire, which was then expanding throughout the Mediterranean lands. In the year 68 C.E. (common era), the Jews started a rebellion. However, two

years later, Roman troops devastated the city of Jerusalem and destroyed the Temple. Many of the Jewish inhabitants fled to other parts of the empire. After another unsuccessful revolt in the year 135, Jews were forbidden to enter the city of Jerusalem.

With the destruction of the Temple, the priesthood came to an end. From then on, the religious leaders of Judaism were rabbis, or teachers, who were respected for their knowledge of the Torah. Over the next 600 years, rabbis wrote down the modern texts of Judaism. The Hebrew Bible took on its modern form, divided into the Torah, the books of the Prophets, and the Writings. The Writings include the "wisdom books" of Job, Proverbs, and Ecclesiastes as well as other literature, such as the Psalms, or Praises.

The rabbis also stressed that there had been an oral tradition, passed down since the time of Moses, that gave more detail on the laws and practices of Judaism. Around 220 C.E., Rabbi Judah ha-Nasi ("the prince") compiled a summary of the oral tradition, called the Mishnah ("repetition"). Later rabbis wrote commentaries on the Mishnah, and these make up the Talmud ("learning"). The Jerusalem Talmud was written down around the year 400 and the larger Babylonian Talmud in 500. Finally, the Midrash ("exposition"), a collection of sermons and commentary, was compiled between 300 and 600. The Bible,

Mishnah, Talmud, and Midrash are the basic sources of Judaism. Sometimes they are referred to in their entirety as the Torah. *Torah* can also refer to the first five books of the Bible.

As the Jews spread throughout the world, they carried these texts with them. Scribes meticulously copied the Hebrew texts onto Torah scrolls. These treasured objects are kept in an ark next to the wall facing Jerusalem in each synagogue, or Jewish meetinghouse. The rabbinical leaders established a public form of prayer in which, over the course of a year, the entire Torah is read aloud. The Mishnah states that a minyan, or quorum of 10 Jewish men, is required before public worship can begin or the Torah can be read. In many synagogues, a hazan, or cantor, chants some prayers and leads others that require communal participation.

A synagogue is not the same as a church. It is not required for prayer or observance of the religion; many rituals take place in Jewish homes and elsewhere. Jews believe that as God's "chosen people," they are required to teach others the laws that God has given them. By example, by good works and charity, and by personal observance of the laws, Jews demonstrate the merits of their religion.

Because the traditional Hebrew teaching is that God created the world in six days and rested on the seventh, Jews observe a Sabbath (*Shabbat* in Hebrew), or day of rest, on the last day of the week (Saturday, in the modern calendar). Observance of Shabbat is required of all Jews. Work of any kind is forbidden.

The Jewish calendar is different from the calendar in general use.

When she left for the United States around 1900, Sonia Friedman Zilbers took with her this photograph of her family in Russia.

By tradition, the Jewish calendar starts with the creation of the world. Rabbis determined the precise year of creation by adding up the ages of the people mentioned in the Bible, therby producing a figure that was 3,760 years before the common era, which in the secular calendar begins with the birth of Christ. Tishri, the first month of the Jewish year, usually begins in September of the secular calendar. The Jewish year 5754, for example, began on September 16, 1993, and ended on September 5, 1994 (5754 = 1994 + 3760).

The Hebrew scriptures and religious texts are the same for all Jews. However, during the centuries after the Jews were driven from their homeland, groups of them developed different traditions. Jews who lived in the Iberian peninsula—today's Spain and Portugal—were known as Sephardim (from the Hebrew word for "Spaniard"). They spoke Ladino, a combination of Spanish and Hebrew.

Around the year 1100, Jews in northern Europe began to be called Ashkenazim (from the Hebrew word for "Germany"). They spoke Yiddish, a combination of German and Hebrew. In time, some Ashkenazi Jews moved into eastern Europe. Beginning in the 13th century, kings of Poland encouraged Jewish immigration by offering Jews protection and religious freedom. The Polish rulers wanted educated and skilled people to help develop the economy, and Jews contributed to the prosperity of what was then the largest country in Europe.

There is really little difference between the practices of Sephardic and Ashkenazic Jews. Both keep the same Hebrew versions of the sacred scriptures and follow the same halakah, or Jewish law, which is a universal part of Jewish tradition.

Customs, rather than Jewish law, mark the differences. The pronunciations, melodies, and some prayers in Sephardic synagogues may be different from those in Ashkenazi ceremonies.

Some of the Ashkenazi Jews who settled in Poland established towns known as shtetls, and in 1551, the Polish king allowed them a degree of self-government. Jews were permitted to elect a *vaad*, or council, which decided all cases involving Jewish law. Officials in the shtetl included the rabbi, the cantor, and the ritual slaughterer who prepared meat according to Jewish religious law.

In other parts of Europe, however, Jews faced harsh treatment. Most Europeans were Christians. Around the year 1200, a series of Christian church councils decreed that Jews should live in separate areas. After that time, towns and cities throughout Europe began to establish separate sections, called ghettos, for the Jewish population. Sometimes these ghettos were surrounded by walls, and residents were required to be inside after a certain time of night. Jews often had to wear a yellow badge whenever they left the ghetto.

Some Christians spread a variety of vicious tales—that Jews kidnapped and killed Christian children, that Jews were responsible for the death of Christ, that Jews practiced secret and horrible rituals that required Christian blood. Jews became scapegoats for many disasters that befell the community. In the 1300s, when a deadly disease known as the Black Death spread through Europe, Jews were accused of causing it by poisoning the wells.

Jews were also resented because some of them prospered as merchants and bankers. Ironically, they were forced into these two occupations because of Christian legal and religious restrictions. In the Middle Ages, Jews were barred from owning land or engaging in agriculture, and they were forbidden to open shops outside the ghetto. As a result, many of them eked out a living as street peddlers. In time, however, the most successful of these roving merchants established trading companies that imported products, such as spices and precious stones, not found in Europe.

Until about the 12th century, Jews served as Europe's bankers because the Christian church forbade usury, or the lending of money at interest. Jewish bankers thus supplied the needs of anyone who needed to borrow money, including kings and nobles.

In 1492, the year that Christopher Columbus sailed from Spain to America, the Christian monarchs of Spain decreed that all their subjects must belong to the Roman Catholic religion or be burned at the stake. Spain's Sephardic Jews were given a choice: convert to Catholicism or leave. About 200,000 Jews were forced to depart from a land where their ancestors had lived for 1,500 years.

After 1492, other Christian states of southern Europe banished their Jewish populations. However, some Jews (known as Marranos) remained by accepting Christian baptism—though a sizable number of them secretly preserved their true faith. Marranos in the Netherlands (a Spanish possession until 1581), England, and France kept the Sephardic Jewish tradition alive.

Tragedy also befell the Ashkenazi Jews of Poland. Between 1772 and 1795, Russia, Prussia, and Austria invaded Poland and annexed much of its territory. Most of the Jewish community in Poland—the largest in the world—fell under the control of Russia. The Russian czars, or rulers, attempted to convert the Jews to Christianity, with little success.

Over time, the Russian government established the Pale of Settlement, where all Jews were

The Reiss family in Germany around 1910. Many German Jews achieved success in business, banking, and journalism and as government officials or university professors.

forced to live. Jewish males, some as young as 12, were drafted into the Russian army, where they were forced to eat pork (forbidden by Jewish law) and to attend Christian services. Sons who went into the army were, in effect, lost to their families because the required term of service could be as long as 25 years.

Jews were often blamed for the backward conditions in which most Russian peasants lived. After about 1870, with the approval of the government, Russians waged pogroms ("outrages") against the Jewish communities, burning the shtetls and slaughtering their inhabitants.

Meanwhile, conditions for Jews in western Europe improved after the French Revolution of 1789. The revolution's ideals included religious tolerance, and in the century that followed, most western European nations began to give legal rights to their Jewish citizens. Even so, progress came slowly and erratically, often interrupted by periods of repression that caused the first great emigration of Ashkenazi Jews to the United States.

Some European Jews had long wanted to return to their ancient homeland. From about the mid-17th century small numbers of them began to move to what was then called Palestine, a part of the Ottoman Empire that included what is today Israel and Jordan. In the late 19th century, an Austrian

Jew named Theodor Herzl organized what became the Zionist movement. Zion was another biblical name for Jerusalem, and Herzl dreamed of once more establishing a homeland for the Jewish people in Palestine. Herzl died in 1904, but others carried on his work.

After World War I broke out in

Around 1908, three generations of the Schwab family of Libau, Latvia, which was part of the Russian Empire, sat for a portrait. Though the grandfather (center) wears traditional clothing, his grandson (right) shows the secular influence of his military service.

1914, however, Europe and parts of the Middle East were enveloped in fighting for four years. During the war, the British government declared its support for "the establishment in Palestine of a national home for the Jewish people." After the war, the Ottoman Empire was broken up into a number of separate countries, and in 1922 the League of Nations gave Britain control over Palestine. Zionists bought land in Palestine to establish Jewish settlements.

Germany, one of the nations that lost World War I, was humiliated by the peace terms. It was

forced to give up territory and pay war reparations to the victors. The German people resented this condition of defeat and began to look for scapegoats. In the 1920s, Adolf Hitler attracted followers to his fledgling Nazi party by proclaiming that Jews were responsible for Germany's plight. After Hitler came to power in 1933, he put his anti-Jewish policy into practice, passing laws that stripped Jews of their legal rights. By 1938, Jews were being sent to concentration camps to be used as slave laborers and as subjects of medical experiments.

Germany invaded Poland in 1939, setting off World War II. By 1945, Hitler had conquered most of mainland Europe and was in the process of carrying out the "final solution," in which about two-thirds of the 9 million European Jews were transported to concentration camps to be killed—a disaster known as the Holocaust.

After Germany's defeat, the ghastly sight of the concentration camps strengthened the Zionist demands for a Jewish homeland. In November 1947, the United Nations proposed a partition, or division, of Palestine into Jewish and Arab areas. On May 14, 1948, Jewish settlers in Palestine proclaimed the existence of a new nation—Israel. After nearly 19 centuries, the Jewish people once more had a land they could call their own.

LIFE IN THE OLD COUNTRIES

After their expulsion from Spain in 1492, some Sephardic Jews eventually settled in Great Britain. Grace Aguilar, who lived from 1816 to 1847, was a faithful member of London's Bevis Marks Congregation, of which her father was president. In her book The Spirit of Judaism, *which was popular on both sides of the Atlantic, she discussed the importance of the Bible and religious training for young children.*

To instruct young children in the dull routine of daily lessons, to force the wandering mind to attention...is far more attractive in theory than in practice. It is a drudgery for which even some mothers themselves have not sufficient patience.... The Bible should be the guide to, and assistance in, this precious employment. There are moments when children are peculiarly alive to emotions of devotion. The Hebrew mother who desires her offspring to say their prayers morning and evening, to abstain from writing, working, or cutting on the Sabbath, to adhere to particular forms and observe particular days as she does, has yet not wholly fulfilled her solemn duty....

All the pious actions...[cannot] excuse...the neglect of the Bible. Vouchsafed in love and mercy as an unfailing guide, it at least teaches what is pleasing in the sight of our God, by the blessings that directly follow or are promised. We learn too "The Lord is merciful and gracious, slow to anger and plenteous in mercy;" that "As the heaven is high above the earth, so great is His mercy toward them that fear Him;" and therefore if the examples set before us in His book are followed according to our ability, aided and strengthened by constant prayer, it is certain we too shall be blessed.

Frederika Dembitz came to the United States in 1849 and married Adolf Brandeis. She grew up in her grandparents' home in Prague, in what is today the Czech Republic but was then part of the Austro-Hungarian Empire. Dembitz recalled:

While the house wasn't exactly elegant in my day, it certainly was ancient looking and unusual and seemed to me very romantic. It played a large part in my life and always helped me to picture to myself what a forbidding fortress must look like....

From the kitchen you went out to the right onto a balcony which was my pride and delight. It had a brick floor, the side walls were as thick as the walls of a fortress, and it was roofed over with brick work. In the middle of the balcony there stood a large old sofa with a faded cover and worn rococo carving.

Rabbi Naphthali Berlinger in Buttenhausen, Germany, around 1930. Study of the Torah and the commentaries on it is a lifelong duty of all observant Jews.

Elazar Behar brought to America this picture of his father and mother, who lived in Beirut, Lebanon, which was part of the Ottoman Empire until 1919. Many Ottoman Jews were Sephardim whose ancestors were expelled from Spain in the 15th century.

My father...was active in the revolutionary movement in 1848. This was an heroic effort on the part of the liberal forces of Europe to achieve constitutional government, and when it failed many of those who had borne a conspicuous part fled to other countries.... These men and their immediate followers constitute one of the most valuable groups of immigrants that have come to these shores since our government was organized. In the land of their birth they had already made sacrifices for constitutionalism and democracy, and basically they had made them for American principles. They were Americans in spirit, therefore, even before they arrived.

A Jewish family in Germany enjoys a trip to the seaside around 1890.

The horsehair stuck out of the cover.... It was my favorite place. Here my mother used to sit and perhaps it was here that she received the first tokens of love from the man of her choice. Here I used to sit with my lover.... The nicest thing about the balcony, however, was the view, for which my elegant friends envied me. In the courtyard below grew a splendid walnut tree planted by Uncle Adolf as a child, which...provided the brothers and their children many a happy harvest of nuts.

The second wave of Ashkenazi Jews came after the 1880s from eastern Europe—Poland, the Russian Empire, the Baltic countries, Romania, and the eastern parts of the Austro-Hungarian Empire. Today, the majority of U.S. Jews are descended from the immigrants in this second wave. Sadie Frowne, who came to America from Poland in the last decade of the 19th century, recalled her family for an interviewer in 1902.

My mother was a tall, handsome, dark complexioned woman with red cheeks, large brown eyes and a great quantity of jet black, wavy hair. She was well educated, being able to talk in Russian, German, Polish and French.... She kept a little grocer's shop in the little village where we lived.... That was in Poland, somewhere on the frontier, and mother had charge of a gate between the countries, so that everybody who came through the gate had to show her a pass....

The grocer's shop was only one story high, and had one window, with very small panes of glass. We had two rooms behind it, and were happy while my father lived, although we had to work very hard. By the time I was six years of age I was able to wash dishes and scrub floors, and by the time I was eight I attended to the shop while my mother was away driving her wagon or working in the fields with my father. She was strong and could work like a man.

When I was little more than ten years of age my father died. He was a good man and a steady worker, and we never knew what it was to be hungry while he lived. After he died troubles began, for the rent of our shop was about $6 a month and then there were food and clothes to provide. We needed little, it is true, but even soup, black bread and onions we could not always get.

Marcus Ravage came to America from Romania in 1900. He remembered the village of his youth in eastern Europe.

The houses were low and made of mud, and instead of hardwood floors the ground was plastered with fresh clay—mixed with manure to give it solidity—which had to be removed every Friday. A family occupied but one room, or two at the most; but the houses were individual and sufficient, and the yard, spacious and green in summer, was filled with trees and flowers to delight the senses.... The pride of a family was in its godliness and in its respected forebears. Such luxury as there was consisted in heavy copper utensils and silver candelabra, which were passed on as heirlooms from generation to generation—solid, substantial things, not the fleeting vanities of dress and upholstery.

Samuel Rosinger served as a rabbi of Temple Emanuel in Beaumont, Texas, for more than 50 years. In his autobiography, Deep in the Heart of Texas, *he described his childhood in Hungary.*

Father earned his livelihood from cultivating a small farm and from the commission for selling the villagers' produce. He had to work very hard to provide for his family of eight children. Mother, however, "looked very well after the ways of her household" [Proverbs 31:27], and efficiency experts could have taken a lesson or two from her.... She sewed, mended, knitted, washed, ironed, cooked and baked, fed chickens, stuffed geese, and milked cows. She was blessed with a sense of scrupulous cleanliness, and our little thatch-roofed cottage was always spick and span. She whitewashed it inside and outside and painted its tamped earthen floor with a solution of black clay, and adorned the center of the living room with a large Star of David enclosed in a scalloped circle. She was the first to rise and the last to blow out the kerosene lamp, even after her five daughters had grown up and relieved her of most of the household drudgery. Mother was a pious soul of sweet disposition who brought up her children with tender kindness and infinite patience, imbuing them with love and reverence for God and training them in the observance of their ancestral faith.

Pauline Newman came to the United States in 1901. She remembered her childhood in Lithuania.

The village I came from was very small. One department store, one synagogue, and one church. There was a little square where the peasants would bring their produce, you know, for sale. And there was one teahouse where you could have a glass of tea for a penny and sit all day long and play checkers if you wanted.

In the winter we would skate down the hilltop toward the lake, and in the summer we'd walk to the woods and get mushrooms, raspberries. The peasants lived on one side of the lake, and the Jewish people on the other, in little square, thatched-roofed houses. In order to go to school you had to own land and we didn't own land, of course. Very few Jews did. But we were allowed to go to Sunday School and I never missed going to Sunday School. They would sing Russian folk songs and recite poetry. I liked it very much. It was a narrow life, but you didn't miss anything because you didn't know what you were missing.

On a Saturday afternoon in the 1920s, Jews in the German city of Baden gather to worship at their synagogue.

Friday evening, the beginning of the Sabbath, in a Jewish home for needy young women in Germany. As in every Orthodox household, the candles for the Sabbath meal were lighted just before sundown.

The celebration of Siyyum ha-Torah (the completion of writing a Torah scroll) in a synagogue in Dubrovna, Byelorussia (present-day Belarus).

As an old man, Shmuel Goldman remembered his home in Poland, where he was a tailor.

Oh, how often in our dreams, like a bird, we fly back to the place of our birth, to that little Polish town on the Vistula.... In this place, the population was nearly equal Poles and Jews. All were poor. There were the poor and the poorer still.

If you walked through the Jewish quarter, you would see small houses, higgledy-piggledy, leaning all over each other. Some had straw roofs; if shingles, some broken. No cobbles on the street, and you might not even want to call them streets, so narrow and deep-rutted from wagons. Everywhere children, cats, geese, chickens, sometimes a goat, altogether making very strong smells and noises. Always the children were dirty and barefoot, always the dogs were skinny and mean, not Jewish dogs. They came over from Gentile quarters looking for garbage and cats. You would go along this way until you crossed the wooden bridge into the main platz. Here were the women on market day, sitting in the open, or in little wooden stalls if they were well-off. Around the platz, a few Jewish stores, a stable, the pump with a roof and a bench.

Most important, you would see here two buildings, facing each other on opposite sides of the platz, without smiling. There was on one side the Catholic church, enormous, two big towers of bells, and across from it, the synagogue, small but dignified, topped by pagoda-like roofs covered with sheet metal.... The church stands there sternly, the synagogue's historical enemy—those two looked at each other all the day. The church was built with splendor inside and out.... The Jewish children were afraid even to look inside.

Young boys went to heder, or cheder—Hebrew for "room," but in reality a school, in a synagogue or the teacher's house—to learn Hebrew and start their religious training. David Blaustein remembered his first day.

That I might not look upon anything unclean on the way, my father wrapped me up in a *tallith* [prayer shawl] and carried me in his arms to the *cheder*, which was about a mile distant from my home. I was received by the teacher, who held out to me the Hebrew alphabet on a large chart. Before starting in with the lesson I was given a taste of

In the 19th century, most of the Jews in eastern Europe lived in shtetls, or Jewish towns, like this one.

honey and was asked whether it was sweet, which of course I answered in the affirmative. I was then informed that I was about to enter upon the study of the Law, and that it was sweeter than honey. After that I was shown the first letter, *alef*, and was told to mark it well on my mind. I was doing that with the greatest seriousness, when suddenly a coin fell upon the alphabet. The teacher informed me that an angel had dropped it from heaven and through the ceiling, because I was a good little boy and wanted to learn.

In 1906, Goldie Mabovitch—later known as Golda Meir—arrived in the United States with her family and settled in Milwaukee, Wisconsin. Later, after her marriage, she and her husband emigrated to Palestine and worked for the creation of Israel, where she became prime minister in 1969. She recalled her early years in what is today's Ukraine.

We lived then on the first floor of a small house in Kiev, and I can still recall distinctly hearing about a pogrom that was to descend on us. I didn't know then, of course, what a pogrom was, but I knew it had something to do with being Jewish and with the rabble that used to surge through town, brandishing knives and huge sticks, screaming "Christ killers" as they looked for Jews, and who were now going to do terrible things to me and my family.

Jews in Russia faced formidable difficulties in getting an education. Elizabeth Hasanovitz, who came to the United States just before World War I, recalled the police harassment of the school for Jewish children that she and her father ran.

Those long years of struggle for an education! At 14 I was already giving lessons to beginners so as to earn money to pay for my books and teacher, so that I might be less a burden to my father.... Many times the chief [of police] and his guards would disturb us in the middle of the day, interrupting our work and frightening the children, who feared the uniforms as if they concealed devils and who were thrown into frenzy at their approach....

After each visit days of misery followed. Many, many times my father and I sat through the night thinking and thinking how to better our condition, what future to provide for my brothers and sisters. Nothing could be done. Members of the human family, people with brains and ambition, we were not citizens; we were children of the accursed Pale....

He would sit downcast, as if guilty for giving life to his children, whose fate like his was to live within the Pale, to be in the hands of the Government dogs, to fear the least drunken moujik [peasant farmer] who, influenced by the priests, would so often make a sudden attack on the property and sometimes lives of the Yiddish people. They said that they considered it a virtue to rob and kill the enemies of Christ.

Freedom, freedom!

Freedom I wanted.

A bagel peddler in Kishniev, in present-day Moldavia. A doughnut-shaped bread, the bagel originated in Polish Jewish communities. Bagels were served at funerals as symbols of the unending round of life.

The children of the Reinitz family in Palestine in the early 20th century. Three of them later emigrated to the United States.

Rabbi Naphthali
Berlinger (upper
right) and his family
in Buttenhausen, Ger-
many, in 1922. After
Hitler came to power,
Rabbi Berlinger sent
his wife and children
out of the country to
escape Nazi persecu-
tion. He remained be-
hind to tend to the
needs of his congrega-
tion, and one daugh-
ter stayed with him.
They perished during
the Holocaust.

THE HOLOCAUST

*Manfred Jonas grew up in a small town in western Germany in
the 1920s and 1930s. He described the changes in his life after
1933, when Adolf Hitler came to power in Germany.*

Hitler's accession to power in 1933 brought some
changes in behavior. On the theory that if we were to
be ostracized and persecuted for being Jews we
should at least understand our Jewishness better, my parents
became active in the synagogue and began to promote my Jewish education. My mother collected money for tree planting in
Palestine, and my father thought seriously about emigrating
there. We became more Jewish—but not more religious.

For me, school began in April 1933. As one of only two
Jewish children (the other was my cousin) in the first grade of
the town school, I suffered both from a teacher who was a
prominent local Nazi and whose son (also in the class) was one
of the earliest *Jungvolk* recruits [a Nazi youth group], and from
classmates who had been encouraged to believe that beating up
Jews made one a better German. A sympathetic principal advised my parents to take me out of the school, and by the following year I was in the newly established Jewish school of the
nearest major city, an hour's train ride away. At age seven, my
cousin and I now lived during the week with two unemployed
Jewish teachers, and enjoyed the freedom of the big city, where
nobody knew us and where our streetcar passes were passports
to adventure.

The school we attended was itself a product of the events
of 1933 and of German-Jewish consciousness. Staffed by teachers fired from the public schools, it was Jewish in its personnel
more than its curriculum. It had a Zionist orientation and required us to study *Ivrit* [Hebrew], presumably as practical
preparation for emigration to Palestine, but the course of study
was certainly secular and decidedly German, with some "Sunday School"—Jewish history and Jewish ethics—added for
good measure.

*Alfred Gottschalk was born in Oberwesel, a small town in the
Rhineland. He recalled Kristallnacht (Crystal Night) in 1938,
when Nazi thugs attacked Jewish homes, stores, and synagogues
throughout Germany. (The name refers to the countless broken
windows of that night.)*

As a child (I was born in 1930), until I was six or seven,
my playmates were mostly Christian, since there was
but one other Jewish child my age in the town.... Many
of my immediate neighbors were Catholics, and although they
knew about Jewish custom and ritual...that knowledge did not

A synagogue in Berlin
set on fire by the Na-
zis on Kristallnacht,
November 9, 1938.

keep some of them from joining in the burning and the ravaging which marked the destruction of our synagogue and stores in November 1938. It also did not keep them from evicting me, six months earlier, from Oberwesel's public school. On that day a Nazi official suddenly entered our classroom and shouted, "All Jewish children out." A little girl, Ruth Lichtenstein (who would later survive Auschwitz), and I, the only two Jews in the class, were unable to understand this sudden expulsion and were escorted out of the classroom while jeers of "Christ-killers"...followed us....

On November 10, 1938...I remember running with my grandfather to the synagogue in Oberwesel in the hours after the great devastation had been visited upon every Jewish community in Germany. It was something the Nazis would call the "Night of Broken Glass," but that Germany's Jews would ultimately refer to as the "November Jewish Pogrom."

There, at the Oberwesel synagogue, I found a blackened, destroyed synagogue interior whose ark was violated and whose *bimah* [the desk where the Torah is read during services] had been hacked to pieces. My grandfather and I found the sacred scrolls of the Torah in the freezing waters of a nearby brook. They had been desecrated into shreds.

After Nazi Germany invaded Poland in 1939, the persecution and extermination of Jews spread. Tanya Shimiewsky, who came to the United States in 1950, lost all her family except her husband in the Holocaust. She recalled for an interviewer the arrival of the German soldiers.

When the Germans came to our town, we were scared in our own houses. Then they made the ghetto. In my town! They moved all the Jews from the whole town together, just in a few streets. And they brought in Polish people from somewhere else and they put them in the houses where the Jews used to live.

We had to wear the Jewish star. It is still always in my sub-

In November 1939, Hitler ordered all Jews in Germany and German-controlled territory to wear a yellow Star of David.

Nazi officers in a German town lead a group of Jews to a railroad station, where they will board trains to concentration camps.

Women in the concentration camp at Auschwitz, Poland, after their liberation by U.S. troops.

Starving prisoners at the concentration camp at Evensee, Austria. Some were used as slave laborers until they dropped from exhaustion.

conscious. When I get dressed, I always look [to see] whether I have it on. It never leaves me. It was a yellow star and black—a yellow patch and the Star of David on it, and *Jew* written there. We had to wear it on all clothes, whenever you went out. If you were caught without it, they put you in jail.

This was in '39. It was very bad. They used to take the men to work. They took them to clean and to do other things.... And one Saturday I heard that they took people, whole groups of people, and they send them out to Germany. And I saw that my husband doesn't come home from work.... I went out and someone told me..., "I might as well tell you. They took Karl in there with the whole bunch." And they sent him away someplace....

I stayed on with my mother and my child—she was then five years old.... And one day we heard that they're going to send out the rest of us, the whole town....

We had to strip, take off all the clothes. There were men and women we knew, and we had to stay in one line, nude. And the doctors marked the people who were able to go to work *A,* and the other people *B....* I had *A* and my mother had *B,* and I knew right away that we're not going to be together....

And I left my little girl with my mother, and she was crying. She was very close to me; she didn't want to stay with my mother. I said, "You're going to be with your grandma. Stay here. Mamma's going to come back right away." I still have guilty conscience that I left her. I always say to myself, maybe I should have stayed with my baby and my mother. And the other mothers with little infants, they ripped out the little children from them and threw them over fences.... You are crying and I not cry.... Maybe we skip this part?

Interviewer: No, please go on.

It was pouring rain, pouring rain, and we were standing all night in this big rain—everybody. And then in the morning they took us to Lodz, and my mother stayed with my daughter and I never saw them again. [Some time later, other people from her town arrived in Lodz.] These people told us that the Germans had open graves, and alive they put them in there and shot them there.

Tilly Stimler, who now lives in West Orange, New Jersey, described what happened to her as a teenager when her family was taken from their home in Romania.

In 1944 we were all taken—my parents, my family—to concentration camps. I lost my parents, a sister and a brother....

My father was taken first. He was like the head of the Jewish community in my hometown and this is why he was taken away before us.... Afterwards I met someone from another town who had been with my father, and he told me that my father had gone through a lot of torture.

Later the rest of us were taken to Auschwitz. We traveled for six days to reach there. I can't explain to you how it looked when we saw it. I think hell will never scare me. We saw the smoke and the Germans, people dressed in leather coats. It was so unbelievable.

As we came off the train, we were told to just go. Then, as I started to go with my mother and my two sisters, we were told to leave everything there. Later my mother and my oldest sister went back to get some things, and I've never seen them again.

Then we were told, "Five in a row, five in a row." So I looked and I saw that my other sister was in the other row. We were taken to these barracks and all of our clothes were taken off and our hair was shaved off....

The biggest impression I have of that day is that it was raining, pouring rain. In May it's still very cold in Europe and especially in Poland. You remember your mother always saying, "Don't go out in the cold and rain; you'll catch cold." Here we were with our shaved heads and in short sleeves, standing in the pouring rain. I remember thinking, "Don't the Germans realize I'll catch cold?" And I remember trying to shield myself from the rain and having a German woman push me. Then I was told, "Don't you ever do that again. She could have shot you."...

We were told later in the barracks that the best thing was to get out of Auschwitz. They said, "You see that smoke? That's the only way you'll get out—through smoke—unless you can get into another camp where they'll put you to work."... We were finally selected to go to another camp, which was smaller and a little better.... We stayed in this camp for several months. Had we stayed longer, many more people would have survived. But as the Russians came near, the Germans made us move. There were no trains, and we had to walk for days in the snow. My feet are still affected from it. Finally we reached Bergen-Belsen.

Bergen-Belsen, as I said, was one of the worst camps. People were dying of disease and hunger everywhere. You just stepped over dead people. In a way, I think sometimes you waited for a person to die so you'd have more room on the bed. We were sleeping so close in a bed that you couldn't turn over. One time I slept in a bed with a person who later died of typhus. Somehow I didn't catch it. I guess that when you are young, the fight for survival must be very strong.

Now, the last few days at Bergen-Belsen were unbelievable. Just before liberation, the Germans brought in more people from the other camps. As they were bringing them in, I saw three girls from my hometown and I called to one of them. I told her whose child I was and she said, "Oh My God. That's you." I told her I was very weak but she made me get up.

She said, "Don't worry, it could just be a matter of hours. Don't you hear the shooting? You know what's going on? We could be liberated tonight." And so she and her friends helped to get me up. I was so weak. But seeing them gave me some kind of moral support. And they were right. The next day the British arrived and liberated us.

As Others Saw Them

Ichiro Imamura served in the U.S. Army in World War II and was one of the soldiers who liberated the concentration camp at Dachau. He wrote about this experience in his diary:

When the gates swung open, we got our first good look at the prisoners.... They were wearing black and white striped prison suits and round caps. A few had shredded blanket rags draped over their shoulders.... The prisoners struggled to their feet [and] shuffled weakly out of the compound. They were like skeletons—all skin and bones....

I saw one GI throw some orange peelings into a garbage can. One of the prisoners grabbed the peelings, tore them into small pieces and shared them with the others. They hadn't any fruit or vegetables in months. They had scurvy. Their teeth were falling out of their gums.

We stayed near Dachau for several days and then got orders to move on. During this time, I found some large chalk-like bars, sort of oval-shaped, with numbers shaped on them. I was about to "liberate" a couple of them as souvenirs when an MP told me they were the remains of prisoners. The numbers were for identification. I put the bars back.

Newly liberated concentration camp inmates at Buchenwald, Germany. The U.S. soldier at top left has helped them build a fire to cook food.

A ship carrying immigrants arrives in New York Harbor in 1906. More than 1.5 million Jews, most of them from eastern Europe, landed in New York between 1881 and 1911.

CHAPTER TWO

DEPARTURE

"No help has come to us!... The glow of shame and quivering wrath overwhelm us when we think of the terrible hair-raising experiences that these last weeks have brought us!... God forbid that we hold our head ready for every blow of the club, that our eye tremble before every flash of our great and small tyrants! It has gone so far that at any hour...there is no other desire in us save to get out of the way."

So wrote Leopold Kemper, an Ashkenazi Jew who lived in Germany, about the persecution that caused him to emigrate.

Between 1840 and 1860, great numbers of Ashkenazi Jews from central Europe arrived in the United States. The Ashkenazi immigrants sought relief from the restrictive laws they faced in their homelands—special taxes levied on Jews, occupational restrictions, and even a limit on the number of Jewish marriages. Many young men left their homeland to escape military service.

This sudden influx of immigrants was also spurred by a series of political revolutions that took place throughout Europe in 1848. Many European Jews had supported these attempts to establish republican governments. When the revolutions failed, thousands of Jews made the decision to emigrate to the one country where their rights were guaranteed.

Whole villages of Jews sometimes left together; people walked or rode in wagons to coastal ports such as Bremen in Germany or Le Havre in France, where they could board a ship for the United States. They brought with them the precious Torah scrolls and other religious objects that were needed to establish new communities elsewhere.

Another great wave of Jewish immigrants followed after about 1880 from Russia, Poland, and other countries of eastern Europe. Conditions for Russian Jews had become intolerable by the late 19th century. The population of the Russian Pale, the area where Jews were required to live, had quadrupled since 1800. Overcrowding in cities and towns, along with restrictive laws, made it difficult for many Jews to eke out a living. After the assassination of the Russian czar Alexander II in 1881 (blamed unjustly on Jewish conspirators), the Russian government and Russian Orthodox religious leaders encouraged pogroms, attacks on Jewish communities.

Persecuted and denied educational and economic opportunities, the Jews of Russia turned their eyes to the "golden land" of America. One-third of the Jewish population of eastern Europe emigrated between 1880 and 1920, and more than 90 percent of them went to the United States. Some left through the Russian port of Odessa, but to do so they had to have official permits, and these

were often denied to families with sons of draft age. Thus, the majority fled their homes in the dead of night, taking only what they could carry, trying to reach the border before the czar's guards stopped them. From there, they traveled to ports of embarkation such as Hamburg, Bremen, Rotterdam, and London.

Jews in Germany and the Austro-Hungarian Empire formed charitable associations to assist refugees who had arrived in port cities with no money to pay for their passage. Even so, most of the eastern European Jewish immigrants accepted whatever space was cheapest in the ships that crossed the Atlantic. Harry L. Barroway, who arrived in 1889, recalled, "The human cargo was treated not a whole lot better than the cattle."

At that time, the sea journey took about one to two weeks. Many Jews tried to bring enough kosher food (which met the requirements of Jewish dietary laws) to last the journey. When that ran out, they often survived on loaves of stale bread, hard cheese, and tea. More modern ships provided kosher food, but many passengers did not trust it. In the stifling, overcrowded steerage, disease spread rapidly. Still, the conditions on ship could not daunt the desperate immigrants. They had endured much worse in their homelands. They dreamed of a new life and opportunity to practice their religion without fear.

LEAVING HOME

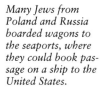

A group of immigrants with their baggage in the Baltic Sea port of Gdansk, in the early 20th century. From 1870 to 1919 Gdansk, called Danzig, was part of the German empire.

Ernst Treu was born in the kingdom of Bavaria in 1839. When he was 17, a letter arrived that changed his life. It came from his brother, who was then living in Keokuk, Iowa. He wanted young Ernst to join him and become his partner. Ernst Treu wrote:

October 21, 1856, was the date set for my departure. It was a raw autumn day, the trees were leafless, the fields bare, the meadows covered with frost, and my heart pensive. My father accompanied me to Schweinfurt, the nearest railway station.... [There] my father spent a little while with me and sought to cheer me by his conversation. When the time for his return trip arrived, he laid his hands on my head and gave me his blessing. Then he took my hands and placed therein his wallet with all its cash, whereupon he embraced and kissed me and then hurried to the carriage, which soon removed him from the sight of my tearful eyes....

I wanted to call my father back to ask him whether I might return home. Then my eyes fell on the purse in my hand. It contained but a few small coins, but for me they were holy, for I felt that my father would as soon have sacrificed his life for me. I pledged to keep the purse faithfully, so that some day I could return it to him filled with gold.

Many Jews from Poland and Russia boarded wagons to the seaports, where they could book passage on a ship to the United States.

In 1880, Yette Beckman of Germany wrote a letter to her son as he was about to depart for America.

My dear Son:

The long-expected has come to pass—your trip to America. You realize, my dear son, the heart pangs I suffer at the thought of your going. It is your wish, and so it shall be. May the Almighty guide and protect you from all evil and always be with you.

Put your trust in Him and He will lead you in the right way. Be brave and good and continue your filial affection. Do not forget our sacred religion. It will bring you comfort and consolation; it will teach you patience and endurance, no matter how trying the circumstances or difficult the trial.

Whether your life be one of success or of struggle, whether rich or poor, keep God before your eyes and in your heart.

You are going out into the wide world, far from parents, brothers, or sisters. It will be trying for you, but you are blessed with many good qualities, and my heart is confident that no harm will befall you. Commit your way unto the Lord and He will bring it to pass....

Though a great distance separates us, and you are far from parental care, my thought of you will never cease so long as my heart beats....

And so, my dear son, I bid you adieu. Write frequently and let me know...what happens to you.... Tears come to my eyes; you will therefore have to excuse my poor handwriting.

This group of Jewish men and boys in Romania was photographed before leaving for the United States in 1900. Most hoped to earn enough money in the new land to bring their relatives over later.

Harry Barroway was born in 1882 in the Russian town of Shklov. His family soon moved to the large city of Pyatigorsk, where Barroway's father was a shochet, *a man who was trained to slaughter animals so that their meat would be kosher. When Harry was about 7, Czar Alexander III issued a ukase, or edict, that forced all Jews living outside the Pale of Settlement to return. Instead, the Barroway family decided to leave Russia.*

We sold or gave away our meager belongings to non-Jewish neighbors, principally the very friendly ones from next door, and commenced our long trek to America, the Golden Land....

Our order of eviction was to leave Pyatigorsk and go back to the Pale where they said we belonged. So-called subjects of the Russian tsar were not permitted to leave [the country] without a governor's passport. This we could not procure.... The alternative means to leave Russia was to sneak across the border at night...and...risk having a potshot taken at us by the border guards.

To reduce the risk as much as possible...the leader of the fugitives...advised the separation of large families, and so my sisters were placed in the charge of a childless couple.

As to the actual crossing of the border, I remember nothing, probably because it occurred in the wee hours of the morning. I may have fallen asleep and been carried by my father to our destination.... After a few days' rest, we bought tickets for

People wait to buy tickets at the Red Star-American line shipping office in Warsaw, Poland.

From the mid-19th century to the 1930s, Hamburg, Germany, was the major port of emigration in northern Europe. The city built an emigrant hall to house those waiting for their ships to leave. This is the Jewish dining room, where kosher food was served.

Hamburg, our port of departure for America.... I remember riding in the train going across the city of Berlin. It seemed to my childish imagination that we were flying in fairyland. The twinkling lights of the street lamps appearing in all directions and my watching from the height of the elevated roof...left an impression on my youthful mind.

For all, waiting for the ship to leave was a trying experience. Benjamin Gordon came to the United States from Russia in the 1880s and later became a physician. He recalled the waiting in his memoirs.

After wandering around the streets of Hamburg for a period of ten days, I was more than glad to see an announcement in the papers that the *Bohemia*, on which I was to sail, would leave Hamburg on the next day. I was ready at the dock so early on the morning of the departure that I was the first passenger to walk up the gangplank and board the vessel. The weather was ideal; the sun was bright and the sea calm; but my heart and mind were not so peaceful.

I knew that I was going to the Land of the Free, but I also was cognizant of the fact that no one expected or awaited me there. I did not have the slightest idea as to how I was going to make a living: I had no trade and was physically unfit for hard manual labor. Then, too, the fact that I was leaving the continent where my ancestors had lived for so many centuries weighed heavily on my mind.

Of course, I was happy to go to America, but to one who has no funds, no trade, and no relations, one of the freedoms in the New World could be freedom to starve. I was rudely awakened out of my reverie by loud blasts of the boat's whistle, signaling the last call for all to get aboard.

In 1893 Mary Antin left Russia with her mother and siblings to join her father in the United States. They stayed at an inn in Hamburg while waiting for their boat to leave. During that time, they celebrated Passover with other Jewish emigrants. It seemed an appropriate holiday for those who were beginning their own exodus.

We were called by the overseer...to the feast spread in one of the unoccupied rooms.... We now found everything really prepared, there were the pillows covered with a snow-white spread, new oilcloth on the newly scrubbed tables, some little candles stuck in a basin of sand on the window-sill for the women, and—a sure sign of a holiday—both gas lamps burning. Only one was used on other nights.

Happy to see these things, and smell the supper, we took our places and waited. Soon the cook came in and filled some glasses with wine from two bottles,—one yellow, one red. Then she gave to each person—exactly one and a half matzos; also some cold meat, burned almost to a coal for the occasion....

When we came to the place where you have to drink the wine, we found it tasted like good vinegar, which made us all choke and gasp, and one little girl screamed "Poison!" so that all laughed, and the leader, who tried to go on, broke down too at the sight of the wry faces he saw; while the overseer looked shocked, the cook nearly set her gown on fire by overthrowing the candles with her apron (used to hide her face) and all wished our Master Overseer had to drink that "wine" all his days....

Then, half hungry, all went to bed and dreamed of food in plenty.

Sholom Aleichem, whose Yiddish-language plays and stories made him famous in the United States, arrived from Russia in 1905. He remembered the saying of good-byes as he prepared to depart.

Well, we're off for America. Where it is, I don't know. I only know it's far. You have to ride and ride until you get there. And when you get there, there's a Kestel Gartel [Castle Garden immigration station] where they undress you and look you in the eyes.

"So, you are going, really going to America?" says our neighbor Pesi. "May God bring you there safe and sound, and help you strike luck. With God everything is possible. Just last year our Rivele went to America with her husband, Hillel. The first few months we heard nothing from them. We thought they had fallen, God forbid, into the sea. Finally they write us, 'America is a free country where everyone is miserable making a living.' Now, I ask you, is that any way to write? Why can't they write like human beings—the what and the when and the how?" Hirsch Leib, the mechanic, says he would never think of letting *his* Pini go to America. America, he says, is *feh* [a Yiddish exclamation like "ugh"].

Now begins a new business—saying good-bye. From house to house we march, saying good-bye. We spend the whole day at our *machetunim's* [Yiddish for "in-laws"], where they give me a seat in the corner with little Alte. They call us bride and groom whenever they see us together. But they don't bother us. We sit there and talk.

"Will you write to me?" she asks.

"Why not?" I answer.

"Do you know how?"

"In America anyone can learn," I say to her, and stick my hands in my pockets. They all envy me for going to America, even Yosie, the son of Henech Vashti with the crooked eyes.

Celia Adler came to the United States in 1914 to join her sisters, who had emigrated earlier. She remembered the last day before departure.

Well, it was kind of a mixture of sadness and gladness.... I didn't know whether I wanted to go or not.... My mother was afraid maybe I wouldn't have any food and so she baked—they call it *zaharas*. You cut a slice of bread and you dip it in vinegar and sugar and you bake it

In the 1930s, as Hitler's persecution of Jews increased, many began to flee to other countries. This 1938 photo shows a group of Jews outside a foreign consulate in Vienna, waiting to apply for travel visas.

HELP RESCUE THROUGH EMIGRATION HELP

שיפט מיט נעראמעוועטע דורך האיאם
קומען צו אונזערע ברעגען!

42 ל

העלפט זיי קומען

ווייוט אייער דערבארמונג הינם
העלפט **האיאם** העלפט
אין דער הילעטער רעטוגנס ארבעט
שנדר'ט פאר האיאם

CONTRIBUTE TO HIAS

HEBREW SHELTERING and IMMIGRANT AID SOCIETY
10 TREMONT STREET, BOSTON, MASS.

After World War II, the Hebrew Immigrant Aid Society organized an effort to rescue surviving European Jews and arranged for many of them to enter the United States.

and this can stay for God knows how long. A bag full of it that she gave me [to take] along. And I had a new hat and I had a new dress and you know it was kind of tempting. What I didn't like was the way my mother cried. I can still see her.

Young men of military age were not allowed to emigrate from Russia. Even the old and children could run into problems from corrupt officials. Many Jews therefore hired guides to lead them to the border. One young man, Alexander Harkavy, remembered:

Our first destination [in 1882] was a small city in Lithuania near the Prussian border.... There we found a Jew engaged in border crossing [smuggling]. We contracted with him to cross into Prussia at a price of three rubles a head. Toward evening the man brought a large wagon which took us as far as the border district. There we got off the wagon, and the man left us...to bargain on our behalf with one of the district's residents.... After an hour, our border crosser returned with a Christian man and both quietly ordered us to come along. Trembling mightily, we followed them. They led us into Prussia. The border area was filled with wells of water and slime.... Finally, after wandering about for half an hour, we came to the city of Eydtkühnen in Prussia. The short time had seemed to us an eternity.

Louis Waldman was born in Russia in 1892 and came to the United States as a young man. He remembered his trip.

Without ever having seen a large city in Russia, although Kiev and Zhitomir were not far from Yancherudnia, I was now on my way across the world to America. I was young, I was hopeful, and for the first time in my life I had seventy-five dollars in ready cash in my pocket. My tickets were paid for in advance, my practical father having made all the arrangements through a travel agent.

The first detour I met on my highroad to adventure occurred at a frontier town in Germany where I discovered that, unaccountably, my railway ticket to Rotterdam had not yet arrived. But, refusing to let that little setback dampen my spirits, I settled down to wait and enjoy my new role as world traveler.

This way station was a clearing center for the hordes of emigrants pouring out of the Ukraine and Russia. While I waited for my tickets I wandered among them and was moved to pity when I found that hundreds were stranded there, defrauded by unscrupulous travel agents. Whole families were completely without funds and without means of continuing the journey. My heart went out to these poor unfortunates and, with a youngster's serene unconcern with money matters, I distributed my wealth lavishly among them.

The days stretched into weeks, until one day I realized that all my money was gone. It was only then that it finally dawned on me that I, the great benefactor, was in the same boat as the other stranded emigrants. My ticket never made its appearance, nor did the disreputable travel agent.

I rallied from this blow, however. A mere lack of money was not going to keep me from America, after I had got that far. Boldly I sought out the head of a travelers' aid organization and told him of my plight. I must have presented a heart rending spectacle, for I walked out of his office generously supplied with money for a ticket—which was all that I, with characteristic improvidence, had asked for.

I had absolutely no money for food on the trip. Somehow I had managed to obtain some bread before I left and this, with unlimited quantities of water, served to keep me alive on the three day train journey from eastern Germany to Holland. I saw absolutely nothing of the cities or countryside through which we passed. I was chained to my seat in the train by weakness and my complete lack of money. When I arrived at the steamship office in Rotterdam I fell into a dead faint. By some miracle, I found the steamship ticket waiting for me.

Before the emigrants could embark on the ship, they had to pass a physical examination. At first the examination was given by the steamship company, which would bear the cost of returning the immigrant if he or she failed the second physical examination in the United States. After 1924, the American consul in the port of departure carried out the examination. One of the most dreaded features of the physical was the eye examination. Fannie Strauss, who left Russia to join her father in Savannah, Georgia, recalled failing this exam.

In 1911, my father...sent for me, my mother and my two sisters. But before we got to the ship they examined our eyes.... I had some problems and I was turned back. So my two sisters went on ahead [with] a couple that agreed to take them on as their children.... I was the youngest, so [my mother] turned back with me.... We had to have my eyes treated, and it took two years before we finally were able to get through.

Celia Soloway, a Russian Jew, left home in 1922. She recalled the examination in the German port of Danzig.

The Germans looked in our heads, hair by hair...for nits [lice]. Now a lot of the girls, the Germans cut their hair off altogether. They made them bald.... My sister, Margie, right away they cut her hair. She had beautiful hair and right away they cut it off. They didn't find anything. But they said it was for safety.

Fannie Strauss, who came to the United States in 1913, remembered that her father had come earlier to avoid fighting in the Russian army during the Russo-Japanese War.

My father came ahead of us all. He came just around the time of the Russo-Japanese War. It must have been around 1905.... He didn't want to fight in the war. If he had stayed there another six months he would have been drafted.... And Jews in those days had very little love for Russia. They were born there and they had to live there, but they certainly didn't want to risk their lives for the czar. So it was either be drafted in the Russian war against Japan and perhaps get killed or make it your business to get out. This is what he did. He had to steal across the border...which meant that he had to pay an agent who, for money, could get you out.

A group of immigrants on board the ship Kaiser Wilhelm der Grosse in 1902. At that time, Jews from Russia and Poland made up about 75 percent of the Jewish immigrants to the United States.

THE VOYAGE

In 1931, an old woman described her trip from Germany to the United States in 1856. With her brothers and sisters, she had traveled by covered wagon to Danzig and from there sailed to Liverpool, England, where they boarded a sailing ship to cross the Atlantic.

We were on the sailing ship eleven weeks. My poor mother was sick nearly all the time.... My mother asked for some food, that she could make a soup or gruel. So the mate...gave her a gruel that was prepared for cats.... My oldest sister, Faiga, cooked the broth.... I noticed my mother bringing up the food as she ate.... My sister could not bring up any of the food although she was given emetics. It had no effects as to produce vomiting. She died that night.... As soon as the officers found she was dead, they immediately took her from us and my mother never saw her again although she begged and implored them to let her dress [Faiga] as becomes one of our kind, but all her beseeching was in vain. The officers and crew threw [Faiga] into the ocean.... My youngest sister, Miriam Rose, who was 11 years old, died the next day about sunset.... I noticed [her] closing her eyes and she was no more.... I can see everything now as then after more than 75 years. [Her sister's body was dumped overboard.] The splash I shall never forget if I live to be 100.

Most of the Jewish immigrants between 1880 and 1920 traveled in steerage, where the lowest-price berths were located. Although allowed on deck to get a breath of fresh air, they were still separated from the other passengers.

Louis Waldman described his voyage to the United States in the steerage of a passenger ship in the early years of the 20th century.

There were some 40 or 50 men, women, and children crowded into one room with absolutely no ventilation other than that provided by the hatchway through which we had entered. Cots were set up in tiers with just enough space between the sets of bunks for one person to squeeze through with difficulty. The odors were indescribable, and breathing was far from a reflex activity; it required actual effort. Baggage had to be kept either on the floor or beneath the cot or on the cot itself. People were constantly stumbling over stray bags and packages.

We ate at long tables and from large bowls into which the entire meal, except for liquids, was dumped. But the foul odors of the ship and of unwashed bodies packed into close quarters were not conducive to hearty eating. In a way this was fortunate because there was not enough food for all. It was only after seasickness began to take its toll that those who could eat had enough food. After starving my way across Europe, at first I attacked the ship's victuals ravenously. But I could not stomach them for long and spent the rest of the trip detesting food and longing for an end to this tormenting journey.

Edith LaZebnik was only 16 years old when she came from Poland to the United States in the early years of the 20th century. She left from the port of Bremen. Years later she wrote:

Finally came the time we should go and we went to the boat. A little boat we took to get to the big boat. *Bremen* they called it. It was in the Russian war with Turkey, a very old ship. It danced on the water like a ballerina. Everybody got sick right away. The bread was so hard we used to throw it in the ocean. We lay in the bottom of the boat and rats jumped over us as we screamed. There was a big storm and the boat was crying like an old woman, oy, in her bones, and everybody was yelling that pretty soon the boat was going to break, and the sailors were running up and down, and water came in through the bottom. That's the way it was on the ocean for 32 days.

Michael Meyer, a professor of Jewish history at the Jewish Theological Seminary in New York City, described how he and his family got out of Berlin during World War II.

My parents remained in Berlin up until the summer of 1941. By now my father was doing forced labor for the huge Siemens electrical company. My mother was desperately trying to get a visa from the stingy American consulate in Berlin. Bribery finally did the trick. We were fortunate since we had relatives in America who signed an affidavit, and my father had a foreman who, when asked to sign an emigration release for him, supposedly said: "Let Karl Meyer too see better times some day."

Pauline Newman came to the United States from Lithuania in 1901. She remembered:

That was the time, you see, when America was known to foreigners as the land where you'd get rich. There's gold on the sidewalk—all you have to do is pick it up. So people left that little village and went to America. My brother first and then he sent for one sister, and after that, a few years after that, my father died and they sent for my mother and my other two sisters and me. I was seven or eight at the time. I'm not sure exactly how old, because the village I came from had no registration of birth, and we lost the family Bible on the ship and that was where the records were.

Immigrants gather on deck with their baggage, preparing to disembark onto their adopted land.

A waiting room at Ellis Island around 1900. Jewish families from eastern Europe often arrived together, and almost one-fourth of all Jewish immigrants in the early 20th century were under the age of 14.

THE GOLDEN LAND

I n September 1654, 23 Jews disembarked from a ship named the *Sainte Catherine* into the Dutch colony of New Amsterdam—today's New York City. Like many of the 3 million Jewish immigrants who would follow in the next three centuries, these early Jewish Americans were fleeing religious persecution.

In 1630, Jews from the Netherlands had helped to establish a Dutch colony in Recife, on the east coast of South America.

Two decades later, however, Portuguese soldiers captured the settlement and expelled about 600 Jews—including those who later landed in New Amsterdam.

The passengers of the *Sainte Catherine* were not the first Jews in what is today's United States. Two Jewish traders already lived in New Amsterdam. There were also Marranos who secretly practiced Judaism in the Spanish settlements of today's Texas and New Mexico as early as 1579. (Indeed, some were burned at the stake for doing so.)

But the newcomers in New Amsterdam would form a Jewish community that has survived to the present day. Congregation Shearith Israel, founded by descendants of those first immigrants, today has its synagogue on the Upper West Side of Manhattan.

Peter Stuyvesant, governor of New Amsterdam, opposed the presence of what he called the "deceitful race" who professed an "abominable religion." Stuyvesant wrote his superiors at the Dutch West India Company in Amsterdam, asking permission to deport the Jews. The directors of the company denied his request. In fact, the company's shareholders included some Dutch Jews, who sent money to New Amsterdam to pay the captain of the *Sainte Catherine* for transporting the refugees.

Nonetheless, Stuyvesant continued to persecute the Jewish settlers by denying them the right to travel, trade, own property, and even to sell bread. Asser Levy, one of the four adult males on the *Sainte Catherine,* successfully petitioned the Dutch West India Company for relief from these restrictions. A butcher, Levy carried on his business just outside the city wall (today's Wall Street) and became a prominent merchant.

In 1664, the English conquered New Amsterdam, renaming it New York, and gradually extended civil and religious rights to its Jewish community. More Jews began to arrive in the English colonies of North America, including some who settled in Rhode Island, which had been founded by Roger Wil-

liams as a haven for people of all religions. In 1763, the Jewish community in Newport, Rhode Island, built the Touro Synagogue, today the oldest in the United States. Other Jewish *kehillot,* or communities, were started in Philadelphia; Savannah, Georgia; and Charleston, South Carolina.

From the beginning, Jewish Americans provided a base of support for those who followed. When a Jewish merchant arrived in the New World, he knew that he could find lodging and fellowship from fellow Jews. Similarly, refugees fleeing persecution were assisted by Hebrew Benevolent Societies organized to help the Jewish poor.

The leaders of these communities were Sephardic Jews, who had come from the Netherlands, Great Britain, and France. The Sephardic form of Jewish ritual was the predominant one in the United States until the beginning of the 19th century. Even so, many Ashkenazi Jews—merchants from central Europe and England—were also found in these early Jewish American communities; indeed, by some estimates the Ashkenazim outnumbered the Sephardim by 1720.

At the outbreak of the American Revolution in 1776, there were still about only 2,500 Jews in the English colonies. The majority sympathized with the rebels, and

Jewish soldiers fought and died for the cause of independence. Jewish merchants, such as Polish immigrant Haym Salomon, provided funds to support the independence movement.

The new nation offered further guarantees of religious freedom. The Bill of Rights of the U.S. Constitution, ratified in 1791, declared, "Congress shall make no law respecting an establishment of religion or prohibiting the free exercise thereof." These words promised Jews and all other groups the freedom to worship in their own way.

During the nearly two centuries between 1654 and 1840, most Jewish immigrants were merchants who arrived alone or with their immediate families. They came to the port cities where Jewish communities already thrived, such as New York, Charleston, Philadelphia, and Baltimore.

Jewish Americans became prominent in the life of the new nation. Benjamin Seixas and Ephraim Hart, for example, were among the founders of the New York Stock Exchange in 1792. In 1826 Maryland became the last state to repeal laws barring Jews from public office. That same year two Jews were elected to the Baltimore City Council.

The Jewish American population continued to increase slowly until about 1840. But during the next 20 years, it multiplied tenfold, from 15,000 to 150,000. By 1880 it had increased to 300,000. The vast majority of these new immigrants were Ashkenazi Jews from middle Europe—German states such as Bavaria, Baden, Württemberg, and Posen, as well as Bohemia and Hungary.

The Ashkenazi Jews who arrived after 1840 faced many of the same difficulties as other immigrants of the time. Ships unloaded immigrants at quarantine stations, where the passengers had to remain until it was determined they were not carrying diseases. Once ashore, the newcomers sometimes fell prey to swindlers who awaited

Besides New York's Ellis Island, there were immigration stations in other cities. This group of Jewish immigrants awaits processing in Baltimore, Maryland, around 1904.

them with false promises of good lodging or jobs.

In 1855, New York State established an immigrant landing station at Castle Garden, off the southern tip of Manhattan. Jewish social agencies were among the organizations that offered advice and assistance to new arrivals here. This benevolent treatment attracted other immigrants and made New York the primary destination for Jews heading for America after that time.

New York's Jewish population increased from about 500 in 1825 to 40,000 in 1860. But other immi-grant Jews established thriving communities in such cities as New Orleans, Cincinnati, Cleveland, Chicago, Milwaukee, and St. Louis. Like many people of all nationalities, Jews went to California during the gold rush of 1849, and by the mid-1850s San Francisco had a Jewish community numbering about 4,000 people.

By 1880 German Jews dominated Jewish life in the United States. Some Jewish merchants who had started as peddlers now owned department stores in the major cities. Jewish manufacturers and bankers had earned fortunes, and many others were prosperous members of the American middle class.

Beginning about 1880, however, a new wave of Jewish immigrants began to arrive from Russia, Poland, Austria-Hungary, and other parts of eastern Europe. Between 1880 and 1924, about 2.5 million Jewish immigrants came to the United States, most of them from eastern Europe. Three-fourths of these immigrants were from Russia. Their descendants form the majority of the American Jewish population today.

The great exodus of eastern European Jews after 1880 coincided with a wave of other immigrants from Italy and eastern Europe. Unable to handle their needs, New York turned over the task of processing the newcomers to the federal government. On January 1, 1892, an immigration station opened at Ellis Island in New York Harbor. New arrivals were tagged with a number and herded from one inspector to another. They were checked for a variety of diseases, including mental illness. An examiner would chalk a code letter on the clothing of any immigrant suspected of being deficient.

Heartbreaking situations sometimes arose when one member of a family was denied entry, and the others faced the decision of whether to divide the family by staying in America or return to Europe with the one who was rejected.

Jewish Americans became concerned about the influx of newcomers in the late 19th century. Many of the families who had arrived earlier became prosperous and acclimatized to American life. By contrast, most Jewish immigrants from eastern Europe were poor, wore traditional clothing, and spoke little or no English. Jewish Americans feared that the newcomers' appearance would cause prejudice against all Jews.

Indeed, Jews from the shtetls faced a very different world in the United States and were sometimes ill prepared to deal with it. American Jews formed groups such as the Hebrew Immigrant Aid Society, which raised money to give the newcomers a fresh start and to educate them about the ways of American life.

The outbreak of World War I in Europe in 1914 temporarily halted immigration from Europe. Afterward, Jews from eastern Europe continued to arrive, as well as some Sephardic Jews from the Balkan countries and the former Turkish Empire. But in the postwar years, the United States began to adopt a more restrictive immigration policy. Prejudice against the large number of immigrants—Jewish and non-Jewish—from eastern and southern Europe was the cause. In 1924, Congress passed a law that set a limit on the number of new immigrants based on their national origin. The quotas were set based

The parents of this group of Jewish orphans were killed during a pogrom in Russia. The children arrived in the United States in October 1900.

on the population of nationals already in the U.S. in 1890. These quotas favored immigrants from the Scandinavian countries.

After that time, Jewish immigration fell to about 10,000 a year, from a peak of 152,000 in 1906. In 1921, just three years before the quota was established, nearly 120,000 Jews entered the United States.

Tragically, these quotas were in place when the Nazi government of Germany began its persecution of the Jews. European Jews seeking a haven in the United States found it difficult to gain admission. On oc-

casion, boatloads of refugees were turned away from U.S. ports, and some of the passengers eventually died in the concentration camps.

Even so, about 150,000 European Jews managed to enter the United States from 1930 through 1941. Many of them were highly educated people who greatly enriched their new country. Indeed, Jewish refugees such as Albert Einstein, Leo Szilard, and Edward Teller contributed to the research effort that helped the United States develop the atomic bomb during World War II.

At the end of the war, the discovery of the full horror of the Nazi death camps created sympathy for the hundreds of thousands of Jews who survived the Holocaust. Congress passed laws that helped refugees to immigrate to the United States, and between 1945 and 1952 about 140,000 Jewish immigrants arrived.

The United States has remained a haven for Jews fleeing oppression and seeking economic opportunity. Many refugees from the Soviet Union arrived here after the 1960s. In the 1990s, the breakup of the Soviet Union and the fall of communism in eastern Europe enabled Jews to emigrate freely, and many have taken advantage of the opportunity. More than 80,000 Jews have also come to this country from Israel. They followed the millions who had led the way since 1654 and became the newest Jewish Americans. Today, in fact, about 4 out of every 10 Jews in the world are U.S. citizens.

Two pairs of silver Torah scroll bells and one pair of silver candlesticks, which was made by the revolutionary patriot Paul Revere.

A Torah scroll belonging to the Shearith Israel congregation of New York City. It was partially burned by British troops during the American Revolution.

The interior of the Beth Elohim synagogue in Charleston, South Carolina, built in 1795. The drawing was made by Solomon N. Carvalho, a Jewish American artist and photographer. The synagogue was destroyed by fire in 1838.

JEWS IN EARLY AMERICA

Bernard Baruch, a 20th-century Jewish American financier and adviser to Presidents, described his Sephardic ancestor Isaac Marques.

Arriving in New York sometime before 1700, he [Marques] established himself as a shipowner whose vessels did business with three continents. He was a contemporary of the legendary Captain William Kidd...[whose] widow lived across the street from Isaac Marques....

It would be colorful if I could claim descent from a pirate. Alas, the documentation I have assembled prevents my doing this. All available evidence indicates that Isaac Marques kept his salt-water ventures on the starboard side of the law. One bit of circumstantial data supporting this conclusion arises from the fact that a year after he became a freeman of the city, piracy suddenly went out of fashion. This was due to the arrival of a new governor...who...launched a vigorous anti-pirate drive. One victim of this campaign was Captain Kidd....

The earliest document relating to my first American ancestor that I have been able to find is dated September 17, 1697. On that day Isaac mounted the City Hall steps, stood before the Mayor and Aldermen of the Corporation, and after due examination and the payment of five pounds, was made a freeman of the city. This gave him the right to vote in local elections. It also required him to serve in the militia.

Abigail Levy Franks belonged to Congregation Shearith Israel in New York City. Her husband, Jacob, was elected parnass, or president, of the congregation in 1743. A decade earlier, Abigail Franks wrote to her son Naphtali, who was staying with her brother in London.

October 7, 1733.

Moses [another son] is learning mathematics at Mr. Malcolm's who tells me he will go through it with an abundance of ease, and be perfect in very little time. Phila [a daughter] learns French, Spanish, Hebrew, and writing in the morning, and in the afternoon she goes to Mrs. Brownell's. She makes a quick advance in whatever she learns. Mr. Lopez tells me he is surprised at her advancement in Spanish. I intend to send for some patterns for her to work upon next summer.

June 15, 1735.
Your sister Richa has begun to learn on the harpsichord and plays three very good tunes in a month's teaching. Her

master is one Mr. Pachelbel. Mr. Malcolm says he is excellent. Moses...profits very much in his drawing and has begun to learn to paint upon glass which he does very well.

October 25, 1737.

I have sent you two kegs of pickles. One is a 15 gallon filled with pepper and the other ten with mangoes, peaches and a few pepper to fill up the cask. When you receive them take the peaches and mangoes from the pepper and put fresh vinager to them and that will take off the strength of the pepper.... I have nothing else but conclude with my prayers for your long life and happiness, dear child.

One of the problems of Jews in early America was their small population. Rebecca Samuel of Petersburg, Virginia, wrote to her parents in Hamburg, Germany, in 1791.

Dear parents, I know quite well you will not want me to bring up my children like Gentiles. Here they can not become anything else. Jewishness is pushed aside here. There are here [in Petersburg] ten or twelve Jews, and they are not worthy of being called Jews. We have a shohet [ritual butcher] here who goes to market and buys terefah [nonkosher] meat and then brings it home. On Rosh Ha-Shanah and on Yom Kippur the people worshipped here without one sefer torah [Scroll of the Law], and not one of them wore the tallis [prayer shawl]...except Hyman [Rebecca's husband] and my Sammy's godfather. The latter is an old man of 60, a man from Holland. He has been in America for 30 years already; for 20 years he was in Charleston, and he has been living here for four years. He does not want to remain here any longer and will go with us to Charleston. In that place there is a blessed community of 300 Jews.

You can believe me that I crave to see a synagogue to which I can go. The way we live now is no life at all. We do not know what the Sabbath and the holidays are. On the Sabbath all the Jewish shops are open; and they do business on that day as they do throughout the whole week. But ours we do not allow to open. With us there is still some Sabbath....

You cannot know what a wonderful country this is for the common man. One can live here peacefully. Hyman made a clock that goes very accurately, just like the one in the Buchenstrasse in Hamburg. Now you can imagine what honors Hyman has been getting here. In all Virginia there is no clock [like this one], and Virginia is the greatest province in the whole of America...

My children cannot learn anything here, nothing Jewish, nothing of general culture. My Schoene [daughter], God bless her, is already three years old. I think it is time that she should learn something, and she has a good head to learn. I have taught her the bedtime prayers and grace after meals in just two lessons. I believe that no one among the Jews here can do as well as she. And my Sammy (born in 1790), God bless him, is already beginning to talk.

Haym Salomon

When Haym Salomon arrived in America in 1772, he was already a supporter of liberty. He had to flee his native Poland because he had spoken out in favor of Polish independence from Russia.

Settling in New York City, Salomon established himself as a merchant. He also joined the Sons of Liberty, one of the secret groups that worked to resist British rule of the American colonies. In 1776, when the Revolution broke out, the British authorities in New York arrested Salomon. Because he could speak German, he was released and used as an interpreter for the German-speaking Hessian soldiers whom the British paid to fight the American rebels. Salomon urged the Hessians to fight on the Patriot side and was again thrown in jail.

In 1778, he escaped and went to Philadelphia, which was controlled by the American rebels. He became a bill-broker, a kind of insurance agent who guaranteed that people's debts would be paid; in return, he received a percentage of the debt. In the midst of revolution, such an occupation was risky, but Salomon established a reputation for reliability, and he prospered. Robert Morris, an American financier in charge of raising money for George Washington's army, appointed Salomon as the bill-broker of the rebel government.

The revolutionary government had, in fact, little money to pay its bills. Salomon pledged his own fortune as security for the loans that were needed to buy supplies for Washington's army. He also used his international contacts to obtain loans from France. It has been estimated that Salomon personally lent $650,000 to support the revolutionary government and army—an immense sum equal to many millions of dollars today.

After the war, the new government was strapped for cash, and Salomon was never repaid for the crucial support he had provided during the Revolution. He died in Philadelphia in 1785.

A customs inspector in Baltimore examines the eyes of an immigrant in 1904. Anyone who showed signs of trachoma, a contagious eye disease, could be refused entry.

These Jewish immigrants were the first to enter the United States through the port of Galveston, Texas. They arrived on July 1, 1907.

NEW ARRIVALS

Jesse Seligman, who landed in New York in 1841, described the process of entering the United States in those days. He recalled the humble circumstances of his arrival with good humor, as he could afford to, for 50 years later when he gave this speech, he had become a multimillionaire.

I t was on a Monday morning that I landed...and at a time when immigrants were in great demand. I soon learned that the government had sent an official to me for the purpose of seeing whether my wooden box...contained anything that would be subject to the payment of duties....

After ransacking the contents of my humble box...the official made a very serious face, and, fearful that he had discovered something that would compel him to retain it, I asked him the cause of his annoyance. He stated that he felt very much disappointed, indeed, in not finding a dress suit among the contents of my wardrobe. I told him that in my haste to get to this land of liberty and freedom, I had overlooked it.

In 1886, 22-year-old Emma Goldman arrived in New York from Russia with her sister Helena.

W e were surrounded by gesticulating people—angry men, hysterical women, screaming children. Guards roughly pushed us hither and thither, shouted orders to get ready, to be transferred to Castle Garden, the clearinghouse for immigrants.

The scenes in Castle Garden were appalling, the atmosphere charged with antagonism and harshness. Nowhere could one see a sympathetic official face; there was no provision for the comfort of the new arrivals, the pregnant women and young children. The first day on American soil proved a violent shock. We were possessed of one desire, to escape from the ghastly place.

Around 1890, six-year-old Harry Barroway and his family arrived in New York after leaving Russia. Many years later, Barroway recalled his first impressions.

A fter a long, stormy voyage of three weeks' duration, we arrived sick and exhausted at Castle Garden, where I remember that the Hebrew Immigrant Aid Society provided us with comforts that we had not seen since leaving Pyatigorsk. Castle Garden was the island in New York used before the Ellis Island era for an immigrant station in New York harbor. I can still remember the receiving portion of the building. The immensity of the room was astounding to me. I had never seen anything like it. Father passed the examination with flying colors. He procured enough cash to purchase railroad tickets for Philadelphia, our ultimate destination, and had the ten dollars over and above, thus complying with the law.

Harry Mesher came to this country from the Ukraine in the early years of the 20th century. When he left, he was suffering from an inflamed eye and dreaded the eye examination at Ellis Island. In 1904, 20,000 immigrants failed it and were sent back to their home country. Mesher recalled what happened when the doctor started to inspect his eyes.

I wouldn't let him. He turned away to talk to somebody and I remember distinctly my sister Bessie gave me a shove on to the next doctor who looked at my throat and that's how I made it. If he had seen my eyes they would have sent me back to Russia.

Rachel Gerson, who came from England in 1921 when she was 12, recalled:

We traveled tourist. That's like third class. We weren't in steerage with the immigrants from countries like Russia; they were on a deck below us....
We landed in New York...but we were taken immediately by boat to Ellis Island where they gave you a thorough examination. Because they wouldn't let anybody in who had trachoma [an eye disease]. And all the heads had to be examined for lice. They really gave you a thorough examination. That was the most horrible place I have ever been.

Fannie Shamitz Friedman spent three nights at Ellis Island because her sister-in-law was sick. Concerts were sometimes held on the island for those who were detained. As Fannie recalled, her father, who had immigrated earlier, arrived during one of these concerts.

We were [afraid]. Because they did send back people. But you can't just worry all the time. My mother, I suppose, worried more than I did. And we...went to a concert. They had all these long benches. We all sat there. For the first time in our lives, we saw somebody in a concert singing to us music, and everybody looked so happy, you know, the people who were already here. And then they announced with the loudspeaker, "The family Shamitz." And we all got up and we ran. You know they were walking in front of us and showed us, and my father was already standing there. And we all came into the office, I suppose, where they let the people get together, and, oh, we kissed and hugged. My father had no beard. That's why I didn't recognize him.

In 1914, 12-year-old Celia Adler came from Poland by herself to join her sisters. When one of her sisters came to pick her up, the authorities at Ellis Island declared that she was too young to support Celia, so Celia had to stay overnight until an older sister could pick her up. Years later, she told an interviewer:

In 1905, this young Jewish woman arrived at Ellis Island from Russia. Her eyes reveal the strain of the journey and uncertainty about her new life.

Sitting on the dock at Ellis Island, this elderly man holds tightly to his basket of possessions. It may have contained everything he managed to take with him when he fled from a pogrom.

The children here are post–World War II refugees from Europe, escorted by workers from the Hebrew Immigrant Aid Society.

These Jewish children arrived in New York in June 1939, just before the outbreak of World War II in Europe. About 150,000 refugees from Nazi Germany were allowed entry into the United States from 1935 through 1941.

The people that remained were very much on the edge because they envied the other people that got off.... They took us in and they gave us a bowl of soup again with a little something as big as this, I think. A roll. That was the dinner. From this room, we went into an empty room with people [who] were already sitting by the wall and their clothes there. On the ceiling, they had hammocks. I slept in a hammock. And you want to know what happened to me with this hammock?...

I walked in, as I said, to this room, and I didn't know where that I am, holding my little satchel. I had a handbag. A friend of mine gave me a small sailor hat, a going away present. The hatpins were that big, that long, doesn't fit on the hat, stands up there. So I walk in with that hat, I pinned my hat...and I walk, like a queen, I walk in that room with hammocks and people sleeping on the floor and whatnot. I decided to take a hammock. But I didn't know that to lie down you had to take off the hat. I had a problem. Don't ask. I was standing by the hammock until some man came from the back, pulled me up, and I remained sitting on the hammock all night because I was afraid to push. If I start moving, that hammock is going to start swinging.... Anyway, at daylight I managed to turn over a little bit and I jumped down from the hammock still with my hat and my hatpins.... I didn't know where the door was, I must have been sleepy or something, until they started to call [us] to go in a line, in all languages. I got there, and then I saw my older sister on the other side of the gate. She had a little girl of three years old on her hands and her identification I guess and papers.... So we got together and we started to walk out from Ellis Island to the pavement where the ships are [to take immigrants to Manhattan]....

In those years, when you came over from Europe, they call you greenhorn.... All of a sudden I arrived and I'm the greenhorn. I held onto my basket, and the hat was pinned up, and she was sure that anyone who will see me will know that I just got off the boat. And she didn't want it. She...took everything out [of my basket] and wrapped it up in a paper, put it under my arm, and she left my basket with my hat there. I'm not exaggerating, but I looked back until I didn't see it any more. It was my whole treasure.

When the ships landed in cities other than New York, quarantine officials inspected the passengers. Celia Soloway, who came to the United States in 1922 from Vilnius in Lithuania remembered her arrival.

We landed in Boston because there was no room in Ellis Island. We were put on an island.... We were quarantined in a prison because there was so much sickness on the boat.... The prison was not closed, however. The doors were open so you could look around. There was a park inside. You could look around the park but they didn't let us out of [it]. And we were surrounded by water.

A lot of people came to meet us, but they wouldn't let anybody go near us. We stayed there for about three weeks. But the immigration meals were wonderful. They used to give us three meals a day, beautiful meals. We never saw food like this in our lives. We didn't have enough to eat in Europe. And they were feeding us cereal with milk in the morning and coffee and such.

Max Teicher came from a town in today's Ukraine as a 16-year-old in the 1920s. As he recalled, he was not fearful when he arrived.

I had twenty-five dollars to show that I could support myself at least for a couple of weeks. And number two, my friend, Max, was supposed to pick me up. And he did. He took the boat to Ellis Island and he picked me up. However, I didn't need him. They examined me and told me, "Go wherever you belong," because I had money. Max took me to Essex Street, and the first thing he bought me was a hat—a straw hat. It was in August.

During the 1930s, when German Jews were fleeing the Nazi regime, the 1924 immigration law made it difficult for them to enter the United States. Carl Cohen and his wife were among those seeking refuge in the United States. But after their ship docked, they were refused admission. He recalled:

Because my wife was paralyzed it was against the law to admit her. Paralyzed people, blind people, anarchists, prostitutes, inmates of lunatic asylums, and people who say "yes" to the question, "Would you kill the president of the United States?" I never heard of anybody answering "yes." Because of this they would not allow my wife to come in, and not me either, because they thought I would abandon my wife. Some such thing had happened before. People got married on paper, without consummating marriage, just to save somebody's life, and I'm not above it. I would have done it, too, but it so happens that I was in love with my wife.

I was there for five weeks. Then I got tired and sick of it and announced a hunger strike and sent a letter to Mrs. Roosevelt, the wife of the president. I lied—that I had a personal relationship to her, an introduction—that I was going to write to her on the basis of this introduction, asking her whether it was a crime in this county to be married to a paralyzed person. Mr. Roosevelt was also paralyzed but I didn't say that. I said all this with tongue in cheek. That evening they got a telegram from Washington, D.C. that they should parole me.

Emma Lazarus

Give me your tired, your poor,
Your huddled masses yearning to breathe free,
The wretched refuse of your teeming shore.
Send these, the homeless, tempest-tost to me.
I lift my lamp beside the golden door!

Few poems have been so widely quoted as these lines from "The New Colossus," inscribed on the base of the Statue of Liberty in New York Harbor. The author was Emma Lazarus, the daughter of a wealthy New York Sephardic Jewish family. She published her first book of poetry in 1866, when she was only 17, and soon began to write plays as well.

Her works won praise from the leading American literary figure of the time, Ralph Waldo Emerson. Lazarus was invited to read one of her plays to Emerson's circle of friends at Concord, Massachusetts. She also translated the works of the German Jewish poet Heinrich Heine and wrote a play about the persecution of Jews in Europe during the time of the Black Death in the 14th century.

It was in 1883 that Lazarus wrote her most famous poem. At that time, the Statue of Liberty was stored in a warehouse. Seven years earlier, the statue had been sent to the United States as a gift from the people of France for the centennial of the American Revolution. However, there was no money to build a pedestal on which it could stand. Moses Lazarus, Emma's father, became active in the effort to raise the funds. Copies of Emma's poem were given to donors.

Finally in 1886, the pedestal was built in New York Harbor and the statue erected. Emma Lazarus died the following year, without knowing that her poem would be immortalized on a brass plaque inside the pedestal in 1903.

This early 20th-century greeting card was printed in three languages and included both Jewish and American symbols. Immigrants from as far away as Russia knew that the Statue of Liberty waited at the end of their journey.

FIRST EXPERIENCES

Adolf Brandeis—the father of Louis Brandeis, who was the first Jewish justice of the U.S. Supreme Court—came to the United States in 1848 from what is today the Czech Republic. Adolf Brandeis wrote home with enthusiasm.

I already love our new country so much that I rejoice when I can sing its praises.... I have gotten hold of a book which contains the messages of all the presidents. This week I have been reading of the progress made in Washington's day, and I felt as proud and happy about it as though it had all been my own doing.... I feel my patriotism growing every day, because every day I learn to know the splendid institutions of this country better.

Joseph Goldmark came to the United States in 1850, after having taken part in the failed revolution of 1848 in Vienna. In a letter to a friend he described his initial reaction.

The first impression of the country is enchanting: the beautiful harbor dotted with lovely islands which with their green hills and pleasant villas delight the eye grown weary of the monotony of the sea. It makes one forget the perils and troubles of the long journey. Animated by new courage, the pilgrim looks upon his new home; its blooming appearance arouses his hopes anew....

The appearance of the city [New York] is very fine; an impenetrable forest of masts [of sailing ships], broad pleasant streets, and enormous amount of business; everywhere keen calculating faces, obviously intent upon their business.

This magnificent, intense life, this wholly unfettered individuality at first makes one breathe more freely, but soon oppresses the spirit of the German unused to such size. The thought of having to swim unaided in this huge stream, if one does not want to sink, is terrifying.

Ernst Treu (who changed the spelling of his last name to Troy in America) arrived in New York in 1856. But he still had to travel by railroad to Keokuk, Iowa, to meet his brother, who had promised to make Ernst a partner in his business.

The railway line terminated at Burlington [Iowa]. From there I had to travel by stagecoach for forty miles. The trip was rough. I sat on the box with the driver, for that was the only unoccupied seat. It snowed and rained, and it was so cold that when I arrived in Keokuk in the evening, I was frozen stiff.

As I left the coach, I looked in every direction, hoping to see my brother. He was not there. I had someone lead me to the home of my Uncle Gerstle, where I was cordially welcomed. There I found my brother, but I no longer recognized him. In five years, he had grown into a tall, strong man. His facial expression had changed completely, and I did not even recognize his voice. What a disappointment!

That night...he told me of his adventures, but of the business, in which I was to be a partner, he said nothing. My uncle and my aunt, however, did not leave me in the dark for long, and soon I was acquainted with the fact that my brother's projected business was merely a figment of his imagination.... Soon thereafter, my brother left Keokuk and settled in a small town in the state of Wisconsin....

Shortly after his departure, he wrote, in response to my inquiry as to how he was doing, "I've got the blues." I immediately rushed to a physician, to ask whether the illness was serious. He smiled and relieved my distress by explaining this psychological disease.

Thirteen-year-old Mary Antin arrived in Boston in 1894. Her father had preceded his family and met them at the boat.

Our initiation into American ways began with the first step on the new soil. My father found occasion to instruct or correct us even on the way from the pier to Wall Street, which journey we made crowded together in a rickety cab. He told us not to lean out of the windows, not to point, and explained the word "greenhorn." We did not want to be "greenhorns," and gave the strictest attention to my father's instructions....

Guide to the United States
FOR

THE JEWISH IMMIGRANT

A NEARLY LITERAL TRANSLATION OF THE
SECOND YIDDISH EDITION

BY

JOHN FOSTER CARR

Published Under the Auspices of
THE CONNECTICUT DAUGHTERS OF THE
AMERICAN REVOLUTION

JOHN FOSTER CARR
241 Fifth Avenue, New York
1912.

The title page of a booklet of advice published for Jewish immigrants in 1912.

A Passover seder at a shelter for immigrants in Seattle, Washington, in 1916. Many Jewish charitable organizations organized efforts to help the newcomers get off to a good start in America.

California was one of many states that established agencies for the protection of immigrants. This poster, from about 1910, was printed in 12 languages, including Russian and Yiddish. It advised immigrants "who feel that they have been wronged, abused or defrauded or who wish information" to visit or write the State Immigration Commission in San Francisco.

The first meal was an object lesson of much variety. My father produced several kinds of food, ready to eat, without any cooking, from little tin cans that had printing all over them. He attempted to introduce us to a queer, slippery kind of fruit, which he called "banana," but had to give it up for the time being. After the meal, he had better luck with a curious piece of furniture on runners, which he called "rocking-chair." There were five of us newcomers, and we found five different ways of getting into the American machine of perpetual motion, and as many ways of getting out of it....

In our flat [apartment] we did not think of such a thing as storing the coal in the bathtub. There was no bathtub. So in the evening of the first day my father conducted us to the public baths. As we moved along in a little procession, I was delighted with the illumination of the streets. So many lamps, and they burned until morning, my father said, and so people did not need to carry lanterns. In America, then, everything was free, as we had heard in Russia. Light was free; the streets were as bright as a synagogue on a holy day. Music was free; we had been serenaded, to our gaping delight, by a brass band of many pieces, soon after our installation on Union Place.

Sonia Walinsky came from Russia in 1906 and later remembered her pride in learning English.

I was six years old and we were on a train with some other immigrants going from New York to Chicago. I had learned a little English before we left home, and I remember when people on the train spoke to me in Russian, I said, "Speak only English. I'm an Americanka now. Don't speak Russian to me. I'm an Americanka."

My brother and I were entered in school in Chicago right away. And my brother, who was ten, was surprised to see me on the stage of the auditorium of the school the first Friday we were there. There was a program, and different children were supposed to do different things, and I was supposed to wave the American flag. I was very proud. I waved it and waved it and waved it with all my might. I thought I was really an Americanka then.

Louis Waldman was born in a small town in Russia in 1892. He came to the United States as a young man and in later years would become a labor lawyer. He described his arrival.

I arrived at Battery Park, New York, on September 17, 1909. Behind me was the bustling harbor with its innumerable boats, the sight of which made me seasick all over again. Facing me, beyond the open spaces of the park, were the tall buildings of lower Manhattan, buildings which were more magnificent and higher than any I had ever imagined, even in my wildest dreams of this metropolis of the new world.

No one had come to meet me, for no one knew precisely when I was to arrive. And there I stood in Battery Park in my tight pants and round hat, with my knowledge of the Talmud,

Yiddish, and Ukrainian, but in abysmal ignorance of English. I wandered around the park for some time, trying to find someone who could understand my language and direct me to 118 Orchard Street, where my sister Cecilia lived. After enduring the blank stares of several park bench idlers I at last discovered someone who understood me, and I was off via horse-car in the direction of the lower East Side.

When I got to the Orchard Street address I had to climb five flights of rickety and malodorous stairs to my sister's tenement flat. It was the first day of Rosh Hashanah [the Jewish New Year] and all my four sisters were there, seated around a festive table. They were at the same time overjoyed and alarmed when I walked in, for I was pale and gaunt from hunger and from the days I had spent below decks. They had known, of course, that I was coming, but my difficulties with the fraudulent travel agent and the delay in Rotterdam had confused them as to the exact day and hour of my arrival.

Sophie Abrams, who arrived in New York around 1920, recalled her first experiences.

My first day in America I went with my aunt to buy some American clothes. She bought me a shirtwaist, you know, a blouse and a skirt, a blue print with red buttons and a hat, such a hat I had never seen. I took my old brown dress and shawl and threw them away! I know it sounds foolish, we being so poor, but I didn't care. I had enough of the old country. When I looked in the mirror, I couldn't get over it. I said, boy, Sophie, look at you now. Just like an American.

Eric H. Cornell fled Germany in 1937. He began writing his memoir, The Lord Is My Shepherd, *in 1982. He died in December 1987, exactly 50 years after his arrival in his "promised land."*

I was deprived from seeing the Statue of Liberty...because heavy fog in the morning not only shrouded her from view, but the whole New York skyline had disappeared, and when we finally landed, all one could admire were the warehouses on 11th and 12th Avenue....

But who cared—certainly not I. My dream had come true, as it had for millions of suffering mankind before, escaping from the dangers of persecution or drought or other scourges.... I belonged to the newest category, the innocent victim of Nazi persecution, condemned because of "Race," notwithstanding the fact that my ancestors were Germans before the majority of the so-called Aryans knew the difference between right or wrong. At that I was one of the comparative few who reached the new Canaan, the Promised Land, the Paradise in disguise, America, and Christopher Columbus or the sailors of the Mayflower could not have been more elated to step on friendly soil.

Wry jokes are part of the tradition that helped Jews survive centuries of persecution. Here is one involving the practice of changing names to more American-sounding ones after arriving in the United States:

Two elderly Jews recognized each other in the street one day. They hadn't met since they were children in Germany many years before.

"Aren't you Avram Silberberg?" the first man said.

"That's right, I was," said the second man. "But in America people call me Abe Silver."

"Oh, yes. My name has changed too. Now I'm Shane Ferguson."

"Shane Ferguson? What kind of name is that for a Jew?"

"Well, you see, when I stood in the line at Ellis Island, I became very nervous. When my turn came, the official asked me what my name was, and I replied "Schoen vergessen." [a German phrase that means "I've already forgotten."] And that's the way he wrote it down."

Arizona pioneer Charles M.
Strauss and his son Charles, Jr.

CHAPTER FOUR

A NEW LIFE

Starting a new life in America meant finding work. From the beginning, Jewish Americans practiced a variety of trades. Asser Levy, one of the immigrants on the *Sainte Catherine* in 1654, was a multitalented man who had many occupations, including butcher, merchant, fur trader, attorney, exporter, and money lender.

Some of the earliest Jewish Americans came to the colonies as traders. Lewis Moses Gomez, a descendant of Spanish Marranos, settled in New York in 1696 and became a major exporter of wheat; he also imported manufactured goods from England for sale. In the mid-18th century, Aaron Lopez of Newport, Rhode Island, owned a fleet of whaling ships. Lopez's vessels also carried cargoes in the trade between the mainland colonies, the Caribbean colonies, and Europe.

There were also middle-class Jews who earned a living as bakers, candle makers, shoemakers, engravers, tailors, silversmiths, wig makers, and dye manufacturers. Many Jews in colonial cities operated small shops. Some English Jews arrived as indentured servants, obliged to work for a period of years for the person who had paid for their passage to the new country.

The numerous German Jews who arrived after the 1830s introduced a new figure to the American scene: the Jewish peddler. Landing in the United States with little money, many of these new immigrants borrowed a small stock of goods on credit and began to sell them door to door. Some left the cities and followed regular routes to small towns and farms in sparsely settled areas.

Carrying their merchandise in a sack over their shoulders, or loading it into horse-drawn wagons, these peddlers were a welcome sight and filled an important economic need. In many of the settlements they visited, stores were few and often sold only farm tools and other necessities. Jewish peddlers brought wares that seemed like luxuries into the drab lives of frontier families. Bolts of colorful cloth, prints, books, cheap jewelry, and a variety of knickknacks tumbled out of the peddlers' packs, making their arrival an eagerly awaited event in areas that were far from any big city.

In time, some peddlers accumulated enough money to open their own stores. Some of the huge department stores and retail chains in the United States began as small Jewish-owned stores. Macy's, Gimbel's, Altman's, and Bloomingdale's in New York City and others such as Meyer and Frank in Portland, Oregon, and Rich's in Atlanta—all are monuments to the industry of German Jewish immigrants. Sears, Roebuck, and Company was only a mail-order catalog business when American-born Julius Rosenwald bought an interest in it in 1895. Under his leadership, Sears became the largest chain of retail stores in the United States.

A few of the German Jewish immigrants accumulated great fortunes, and their careers are among the great American success stories. The Seligman brothers, immigrants from Bavaria in the early 1840s, pooled their earnings as peddlers and opened a wholesale clothing business in New York. Jesse Seligman went to California in 1850 and increased the family fortune by trading in gold. The brothers then opened the banking firm of J. & W. Seligman in New York City. It financed the construction of railroads, the Panama Canal, and public utilities in many cities. The Seligmans helped their adopted country during the Civil War by selling $200 million worth of U.S. government bonds in Europe.

There were other such stories. The Guggenheim banking family began as peddlers in the coalfields of Pennsylvania. Solomon Loeb, a former peddler, and Abraham Kuhn, a cloth manufacturer in Cincinnati, started the banking firm of Kuhn, Loeb, & Co. in the 1860s. It gave immigrant Jacob Schiff his first job in America. Schiff, as head of the firm, became one of the wealthiest Jewish Americans and used his fortune and influence to assist eastern European Jews in the next great wave of immigration.

Eastern European immigrants who started to arrive in large numbers around 1880 outnumbered their German Jewish predecessors by at least 10 to 1. The vast majority settled on the Lower East Side of New York City, where they lived in overcrowded and unhealthy conditions. Jewish social service agencies, both in the United States and Europe, tried to send the newcomers to other American ports, such as Galveston, Texas, and settle them on farms. Nearly all such projects failed, however, mainly because Jews had little experience with farming in Europe.

Like other immigrants of the late 19th and early 20th centuries, many eastern European Jews took menial jobs as unskilled laborers. Those who had practiced trades in the old country found work as watchmakers, carpenters, furriers, bricklayers, shoemakers, butchers, and bakers.

Many eastern European Jews found work as laborers in the rapidly growing garment trade. Control of this industry was in fact largely in the hands of German Jews, who owned 234 of New

York City's 241 garment factories in 1885. But conditions in the factories often were brutal. Children as well as adults worked long hours; others took home cloth to be sewed into garments, for which they were paid by the piece. Safety standards were low, and workers were frequently maimed by the machinery. In 1911, a fire in the Triangle Shirtwaist Factory in New York killed 147 people, mostly young women, because exit doors had been locked to keep the workers from sneaking outside.

Many Jewish women and children worked in the garment industry. Some found jobs in factories, and others took cloth home to sew it into garments.

Jewish immigrants were among the leaders of the labor union movement. English-born immigrant Samuel Gompers was one of the founders of the American Federation of Labor (AFL) in 1886 and served as its president for all but one year until his death in 1924. However, the AFL was a federation of workers in skilled trades, and Gompers had little sympathy for the plight of unskilled workers, which included many eastern European Jewish immigrants.

The growing numbers of eastern European Jewish Americans

brought a new fervor to labor organizing. Before they emigrated, some Jews had become part of the socialist movement and were stirred by its ideals of equality and justice for workers. In 1888, United Hebrew Trades was formed—the first nationwide organization to meet the needs of Jewish workers. Twelve years later, the International Ladies' Garment Workers Union (ILGWU) was founded, with chapters in four cities. The mood of its members, most of whom were Jewish, is indicated by the fact that they called 189 strikes in the next two years—and won their demands in 158 of them. By 1904, the ILGWU had expanded to 66 chapters in 27 cities.

The members of the ILGWU were mostly young women, aged 16 to 25. One of them, Clara Lemlich, rose at a meeting in New York City in 1909 and called for a general strike to demand higher wages and better working conditions. Some 20,000 workers, including Italians as well as Jews, responded at more than 500 factories. The "uprising of 20,000" lasted through the cold winter of 1909–10. Shop owners hired *shtarker* (thugs) to attack the pickets, and police arrested hundreds of strikers. A partial victory, in which about 300 employers agreed to the union's demands, ended the strike in February 1910.

But that was just the beginning. In the spring of 1910, an even larger strike began in New York City among other garment workers. This so-called Great Revolt was finally settled through the mediation of a Jewish attorney from Boston, Louis D. Brandeis, known as the "people's attorney" because he often charged no fee for defending the rights of poor people. The employers accepted a 50-hour work week, 10 paid holidays, higher pay for overtime, and a committee to monitor working conditions.

Chicago's garment workers, inspired by the success of the New York strikes, raised their own picket lines in 1910. After this strike failed, a group of workers led by a Lithuanian-born Jew, Sidney Hillman, founded the Amalgamated Clothing Workers of America. Hillman and Russian Jewish immigrant David Dubinsky (who headed the ILGWU from 1932 to 1966) became two of the most influential union leaders of the 20th century.

At work and in daily life, Jews have faced prejudice—called anti-Semitism because Hebrew is a Semitic language. In the early to mid-19th century, anti-Jewish pamphlets made their appearance, and ads for jobs sometimes read, "No Jews wanted." Around 1870, anti-Semitism began to increase, in large part because of the economic success of some Jews. Jewish Americans began to find they were not welcome in some socially prominent circles. In 1877, millionaire Joseph Seligman and his family were turned away from the Grand Hotel in the fashionable resort of Saratoga, New York—even though they had stayed there many times before. The hotel had a new policy:

it did not admit "Israelites."

It was the eastern European Jews, however, who suffered the most pervasive bigotry. As a group, they were poorer than the Jewish immigrants who had arrived earlier—and there were many more of them. Clustered in the big cities, the eastern European Jews' clothing and language marked them as "different." Vicious cartoons and performers in theaters created the image of a "typical" Jew. In the words of an anonymous hate pamphlet, Jews could be identified "by

Workers at the Boston Matzo Baking Company in 1894.

their hooked noses, restless eyes, elongated ears, square nails, flat feet, round knees, and soft hands." In 1908 the police commissioner of New York declared that "perhaps half" of the city's criminals were "Hebrews."

A public outcry forced the police commissioner to retract his statement. But in rural areas of the South and Midwest, such attitudes were widespread. The Ku Klux Klan, originally an antiblack group, targeted Jews for its vicious activities as well. In 1913 Leo Frank, the owner of a pencil factory in Atlanta, was convicted of

murdering a young girl who worked for him. Because the evidence against Frank was obviously weak, the governor of Georgia commuted his death sentence to life imprisonment. A mob dragged Frank from a prison farm and lynched him. That same year, the Anti-Defamation League (ADL) was formed to fight anti-Semitism and prejudice against all American minority groups.

Even the eagerness of the Jews to succeed through education and hard work was held against them. Jewish Americans faced so-called "gentlemen's agreements" that barred them from upper-class neighborhoods and clubs as well as from many businesses and law firms. Some universities set quotas that limited the number of Jewish students.

Henry Ford, the automobile magnate, spread anti-Semitic propaganda in his newspaper, the *Dearborn Independent*. Among the libels he printed was the accusation that Jewish bankers controlled world finance. In the 1930s, a Detroit priest, Father Charles Coughlin, preached on his nationwide radio program that Jewish bankers had caused the depression. Coughlin also blamed Jewish communists—seeing no contradiction in the fact that communists and bankers were unlikely allies.

In the post–World War II years, most social restrictions against Jews gradually disappeared. Yet anti-Semitism remains, despite the enormous contributions of Jewish Americans to the nation over the past 350 years.

MAKING A LIVING

Hester Street, in the heart of the Lower East Side in Manhattan, was a busy shopping district. All one needed to go into business was a supply of goods and a place to display them.

A boy delivering boxes that probably contain hats. Because there were no child labor laws until the 1930s, immigrant children often worked to help support their families.

William Frank arrived in New York from Germany in 1840. He described how relatives and friends from the old country helped the newcomers become established.

Here again I had a cousin living by the name of Frank. I hunted him up and remained with him overnight. He loaned me $3 with which to reach Philadelphia, where my stepbrother, Phillip Frank, lived. He was a shoemaker and had several journeymen working for him. He had a nice business but was a poor manager, and his wife could spend more than three men could earn. He had made his start by peddling merchandise and had about four dollars' worth of odds and ends in a handkerchief, which he gave me to sell. I remained in Philadelphia seven weeks and purchased additional goods each day. [I] paid my lodging, $3 per week, to my sister-in-law....

During three weeks I made the acquaintance [of] and purchased goods from Blum & Simpson, who gave me credit for goods to the extent of $100, to go peddling out of the city. I peddled in Lancaster County [Pennsylvania] one year and sent my parents $700, for them and my sister Babet and brother Moses to come to America with. They came, but my sainted mother lived only six months after arrival.

Abraham Kohn came to the United States from Germany in the first half of the 1840s. Peddling was often the only road to success and yet it was a hard and lonely life. His journal shows the difficulties.

This week I went, together with my brother Juda, from Boston to Worcester [Massachusetts]. We were both delighted, for the trip was a welcome change from our daily, heavy work. Together we sat in the grass for hours, recalling the wonderful years of our youth. And in bed, too, we spent many hours in talking....

Thursday was a day of rest owing to twelve inches of snow. On Friday and Saturday business was very poor, and we did not take in $2 during the two days.

On Sunday we stayed with Mr. Brown, a blacksmith, two miles from Lunenburg. Both of us were in a bitter mood, for during the whole week of driving about in the bitter cold we had earned no money. I long for the beautiful days in my beloved homeland. Will they ever return? Yes, a secret voice tells me that all of us will again find happiness and, although there are many obstacles to be overcome, the old maxim will guide me!...

Last week in the vicinity of Plymouth I met two peddlers, Lehman and Marx. Marx knew me from Furth, and that night we stayed together at a farmer's house. After supper we started singing while I felt melancholy and depressed. O, how I thought of my dear mother while I sang!...

Dear, good mother, how often I recall your letters, your advice against going to America: "Stay at home; you can win success as well in Germany." But I would not listen; I had to come to America. I was drawn by fate and here I am, living a life that is wandering and uncertain....

It is hard, very hard indeed, to make a living this way. Sweat runs down my body in great drops and my back seems to be breaking, but I cannot stop; I must go on and on, however far my way lies....

Here in the land of the free, where every child, every human being, preaches and enjoys liberty, it is I who am compelled to follow such a trade, to devote myself to so heavy and difficult a life. Each day I must ask and importune some farmer's wife to buy my wares, a few pennies worth. Accursed desire for money, it is you that has driven the Bavarian immigrants to this wretched kind of trade! No, I must stop this business, the sooner the better.

The Abraham and Straus stores used horse-drawn delivery wagons in the 1890s. Abraham Abraham, the store's founder, started with a small dry goods shop in 1865. By the time of his death in 1911, his stores did a yearly business of $13 million.

Henry Seessel went to New Orleans around 1843. He soon started to work as a traveling peddler with his brother, who had established a route in Mississippi.

I did not relish the work of peddling at all. Every time we stopped at a farm to sell goods I had to pack the heavy packages in and out of the houses, and while my brother was selling goods, I stood and watched on the outside, so no one would steal anything.

It was very easy in those days to sell goods. There were no stores at every crossroad. There were stores only in the towns. The eating did not suit me, as I was not used to eating American dishes, such as hot bread, turnip greens, and pork. The walking of from ten to twenty miles per day I did not relish, either.... We made our first trip and sold out in two weeks. I suppose we had no less than five hundred dollars' worth of goods; besides my brother carried a jewelry box, out of which he sold a good deal.

German immigrant Louis Gratz was working as a peddler in Pennsylvania when the Civil War began. In a letter to relatives in Poland, Gratz told how he became an officer in the Union Army.

Business came to a standstill...and after the call of the President to defend the country with arms, all the young folks flocked to the colors. Carried away by the general enthusiasm, I became a soldier. I studied English with great zeal until I could talk fairly fluently. Since I had the good will of my superiors, I became a noncommissioned officer in a few weeks. However, the way to a higher position was barred to me, because I had to write and read English perfectly to get

In 1907, at age 21, Abraham Roth came to the United States from Galicia and settled in Pittsburgh. Around 1920 he used this car to deliver cigars to customers. Roth later opened other businesses, including a dry cleaner and a carpet company.

Adelson's Grocery Store on Thames Street in Newport, Rhode Island, in the 1920s.

The Calvo family, who were Sephardic Jews, owned the Waterfront Fish and Oyster Company in Seattle, Washington. The Sephardic community in Seattle is the largest in the United States outside New York City.

such an appointment. I started again, sometimes studying through the better part of the night, and all this without any help, since I did not have enough money to hire a tutor. Now I am able to speak, read, and write English well. In the meantime, our enlistment term, fixed for a period of four months, expired. Everybody had believed that this war would last only four months.... However, the war was far from being finished, and therefore the President issued a second proclamation asking for soldiers for a period of three years....

Possibly...because of the fact that I had shown courage several times during my first enlistment, I was introduced to Secretary of War Cameron and was examined by him. I had used my time profitably to study military tactics whenever I had a moment, and so I became a first lieutenant in the cavalry of the United States.

In his native Vienna, Austria, Jacob Berger had seen in the window of a shop a book about the Golden Gate Bridge in San Francisco. The shop owner let him have the book in return for sweeping out the store. The book inspired Berger to emigrate to America in 1880, when he was about 17. His son-in-law, Henry Wolens, described Berger's career.

When he arrived in New York, he went to work in a packing shed, packing tomatoes. It was down near the wharf. He had one thing in mind and that was to get to San Francisco. When he thought he had sufficient funds saved up, unable to speak English well, he went to the ticket office and said, "San Francisco." He took the money that he had been saving for several months and put it on the counter. The ticket agent gave him his ticket.... He was penniless, because he had given everything he had for his ticket. The second morning [on the train] the conductor [woke] him, indicating it was time for him to get off the train.... A stranger came by and recognized that he was an immigrant.... Dad Berger told him he had just gotten there that morning. He told him of his dream of getting to San Francisco and now he was finally here. He was thankful to the Almighty that he was in San Francisco. The stranger told him that he...was in St. Louis. Of course, he was very disappointed and depressed.

The stranger was Jewish, and he offered to take him to a good family. He...told them the story. They made provision for him. He had to have a job. They thought he was too young to peddle, so they decided to make him a shine boy. They arranged for a stand for him across from one of the big banks there in St. Louis. He had a charming personality, and people at the bank who came to get their shoes shined were infatuated with him. So, he started out as a runner [an errand boy], and after 20 years, he became a vice president of the bank.

[In 1952, when Berger was around 90, his daughter and son-in-law arranged for him and his wife to make the trip to San Francisco.] He required a wheelchair in moving about, but we had to satisfy the dream he had had since childhood.

In his autobiography, Louis Waldman, who went to New York as a young man in 1909, described finding his first job.

My sisters told me where the various factories were located and all I had to do was to go from door to door to find out whether anyone could use my services.

Finally I stumbled across a chandelier factory on Canal Street which proclaimed on a crudely painted sign—but in three languages—that a "hand" was wanted inside. I walked up several flights of stairs and finally spoke to the foreman. He looked me over, and made careful note of my husky appearance, and told me I could start working. My salary was to be two dollars a week, but he added: "Don't worry, there's room for advancement." Five months later when I quit I was still getting two dollars a week....

I worked at a press which bent a strip of metal into a ring. My job was to keep feeding my hungry, clattering machine strip after strip of metal. The tempo of work was set with complete disregard to myself. I had no control over the speed with which the press came down. If I failed to feed it at the rate to which it was regulated, this fact immediately became known, for if the metal was not inserted in time the press descended with a loud, hollow telltale clang which could be heard throughout the shop. The foreman checked on our work by continually passing along the row of machines and closely watching the size and pile of rings which accumulated at the side of each press.

There were about one hundred men and women who worked in this hot, noisy loft. And we worked from seven in the morning until six at night with half an hour off for lunch. But this ten-and-a-half hour day seemed much longer than it really was because of the monotonous clang of the machine and the unvarying routine of my work.

Mary Antin, who arrived in Boston in 1894 when she was 13, recalled the grocery store her family opened in Chelsea, just north of Boston.

In Chelsea, as in Boston, we made our stand in the wrong end of the town. Arlington Street was inhabited by poor Jews, poor Negroes, and a sprinkling of poor Irish. The side streets leading from it were occupied by more poor Jews and Negroes. It was a proper locality for a man without capital to do business. My father rented a tenement with a store in the basement. He put in a few barrels of flour and of sugar, a few boxes of crackers, a few gallons of kerosene, an assortment of soap of the "save the coupon" brands; in the cellar, a few barrels of potatoes, and a pyramid of kindling-wood; in the showcase, an alluring display of penny candy. He put out his sign, with a gilt-lettered warning of "Strictly Cash," and proceeded to give credit indiscriminately. That was the regular way to do business on Arlington Street. My father, in his three years' apprenticeship, had learned the tricks of many trades. He knew

The shops of the Lower East Side in New York used "pullers" to encourage customers to come in. Barney Ross, who was later a champion boxer, worked as a puller and he recalled:

Whenever a potential customer got close enough for me to get my hands on him, I would seize him and "pull" him inside. The approved technique was not to grab him so hard that you'd tear his clothes, but to get a good enough grip so he couldn't slip out from under.... If he told me, "I haven't got time, I have to go," I'd tell him, "Two seconds, two seconds, it won't take more, that I swear to you on the honor of my forefathers." If he said, "I have no money, I can't buy," I'd assure him, "Forget about money, this'll cost you nothing, practically nothing." If he said "I've got ten sweaters already," I'd tell him, "Listen, you need one real *heavy* sweater...it'll save you money, you won't have to buy a coat."

In 1892, Isaac Cooper and Aaron Levy opened a store in Seattle that sold supplies to prospectors on their way to Alaska.

Sadie Klein and her son Saul in front of their tobacco and stationery store in East Pittsburgh, Pennsylvania, around 1914. The sign over the door reads *Magyar Uzlet*, or "Hungarian business."

Isaac Woolf's factory-workshop in Providence, Rhode Island, around 1900. Woolf and his employees made stone carvings and metal decorations for building exteriors.

when and how to "bluff." The legend of "Strictly Cash" was a protection against notoriously irresponsible customers; while none of the "good" customers, who had a record for paying regularly on Saturday, hesitated to enter the store with empty purses.

If my father knew the tricks of the trade, my mother could be counted on to throw all her talent and tact into the business. Of course she had no English yet, but as she could perform the acts of weighing, measuring, and mental computation of fractions mechanically, she was able to give her whole attention to the dark mysteries of the language.... In this she made such rapid progress that she soon lost all sense of disadvantage, and conducted herself behind the counter very much as if she were back in her old store in Polotzk [in Russia]. It was far more cozy than Polotzk—at least, so it seemed to me; for behind the store was the kitchen, where, in the intervals of slack trade, she did her cooking and washing. Arlington Street customers were used to waiting while the storekeeper salted the soup or rescued a loaf from the oven.

One could make a living by providing services to the Jewish community. Irving Mittleman described his father's work in the North End of Providence, Rhode Island.

There were a number of Kosher butchers in the area. My father and his two brothers all had butcher shops on Chalkstone Avenue. All the butchers were able to make a living, for the Jewish population was there and they all used Kosher meat. Deliveries were all done by foot at the beginning but then my father got a wagon. Meat was kept cold by the ice which was brought in every day or every other day. The meat came in daily, except Saturday or Sunday.... Women had to really cook the quality of beef sold in those days. When it came to a holiday, say, over a three-day period, the women would bring their cooked meats to the store to storage it there.... It cost my father $40 to set up his store. The butcher block was a trunk of a tree.

Harry Germanow, who immigrated from Pinsk around 1909, when he was 18, found factory work in Philadelphia. Later, he became a successful manufacturer, but in his autobiography he recalled the hard times at the beginning.

After several days of knocking myself out from one place to another, I accepted a job at Baldwin Locomotive Works for $9 per week. I worked there for two weeks and did not like it. The building was 8 or 10 stories high. The ceilings were very low. The machines were very crowded and dangerous. People were getting hurt every day, so I quit and got a job at Crane Shipyards for $9 a week. The place was an hour's walk from where I stayed. I walked back and forth every day to save 20 cents car fare.

One morning, about 10 o'clock, I met with an accident. Working on a drill press trying to change a belt from a slow speed to a faster one, my second finger of my right hand caught in open gears and chopped a piece of my finger off. In those days machines were not guarded [had no safety shields] as [they are] now. There were no labor inspectors. I was taken to a hospital where my finger was trimmed and bandaged. I was paid for the day's work till 10 o'clock only.

Ephraim E. Lisitzky, born in Russia in 1885, moved to Boston when he was 15. Later in life, Lisitzky would become well known for the poetry he wrote in Hebrew, but his first thought was earning a living in his new country. He decided to try peddling.

I talked to one of my acquaintances, a boy my own age, who was a peddler himself, and he consented to lend me for a day his notions basket with the understanding that we would share the profits. I chose Tuesday, a lucky day in Jewish tradition, to embark on my peddling experiment.

It was a rainy autumn day. The wind shook my basket and whipped the shoelaces dangling from my hand into my face. I trudged down the street like a doomed man on his way to the gallows. Whenever anybody looked at me I lowered my eyes in shame. I approached a house whose number was the numerical equivalent of a verse in Scripture I had in mind, timidly mounted the stairs—and couldn't bring my hand to knock at the door. At last I knocked diffidently. The door opened. I stood in the doorway with downcast face, and inquired clumsily in a low voice:

"Maybe the lady wants matches?"

"Matches?" The woman at the door responded sardonically. "Come in and I'll show you the piles of matches the peddler already supplied me with—enough to burn up all the houses in Boston!"

I tried to ask her if she wanted any of the other notions in my basket, but I couldn't find my voice. I went down the stairs, bowed and beaten, and trudged along....

"You *schlemiel* [fool]!" I scolded myself. "First principle of peddling, you must be aggressive, bold and talkative, and you mustn't let a customer go just because he doesn't need or want your merchandise—you have to make him want it, keep after him until he says, 'I'll take it!' Ask a woman if she needs what you're selling, you can be sure, she won't touch it. 'Lady! I see that you need such and such, and I can give it to you for next to nothing—' That's the way to talk to a customer!"

I...went up to another house, and knocked at the door energetically, loud enough to waken the dead. The door opened and before me stood a woman with a sooty face and dirty hands who had left her stove to find out what all the pounding was about. I made myself aggressive, bold and talkative:

"I see, madam, that your face is sooty and your hands are dirty and they need a good washing with soap—not just ordinary soap, but a good soap. I have just that, here in my basket, and you can have it for next to nothing. As the prophet Isaiah said: 'And I will cleanse as with soap thy—'" The door slammed in my face! I never finished the verse.

Adolph S. Ochs

In 1869, 11-year-old Adolph S. Ochs, the son of immigrants from Germany, took a job delivering newspapers in Knoxville, Tennessee. For the next 66 years, the newspaper business was his life, as Ochs moved from the bottom to the top of the industry.

When Ochs was 20, he borrowed $250 to purchase the *Chattanooga Times,* which was on the verge of bankruptcy. Under his direction, the newspaper gained circulation and became profitable. In 1896, Ochs boldly acquired control of another failing newspaper, the *New York Times.*

When Ochs took over the *Times,* it had a circulation of 9,000 and was losing $1,000 a day. By contrast, some competing New York newspapers sold more than a million copies a day. Ochs disliked the sensational "yellow journalism" that had brought success to his competitors. Adopting the slogan "All the News That's Fit to Print," he set out to publish a newspaper that would contain an accurate record of national and world news.

Ochs's vision produced what is today the most influential newspaper in the world. Within three years, the newspaper's rising circulation and advertising helped it turn a profit. In 1918, it received the first Pulitzer Prize gold medal for meritorious public service, an award established in the will of another Jewish American newspaper publisher, Joseph Pulitzer.

Ochs also made his newspaper a cultural influence by starting a book review section and adopting extensive coverage of the arts. By the time of his death in 1935, the *Times* had news bureaus in cities around the world.

Since then, Ochs's family has kept control of the *Times,* preserving his motto and goals. The *Times* now publishes a national edition and has survived competition from radio and television. Adolph S. Ochs's great-grandson, Arthur Ochs Sulzberger, Jr., is today the publisher.

THE GARMENT TRADE

Unskilled immigrants took menial jobs such as delivering garments.

In both Germany and eastern Europe, one of the traditional Jewish occupations had been clothing manufacture. Countless Jewish immigrants found work in that industry in the United States— among them many women and young girls. Pauline Newman, who came from Lithuania in 1901, went to work as a child in New York City's Triangle Shirtwaist Company.

A cousin of mine worked for the Triangle Shirtwaist Company and she got me on there in October of 1901. It was probably the largest shirtwaist factory in the city of New York then. They had more than 200 operators, cutters, examiners, finishers. Altogether more than 400 people on two floors....

What I had to do was not really very difficult. It was just monotonous. When the shirtwaists were finished at the machine there were some threads that were left, and all the youngsters—we had a corner on the floor that resembled a kindergarten—we were given little scissors to cut the threads off. It wasn't heavy work, but it was monotonous, because you did the same thing from seven-thirty in the morning till nine at night.

Well, of course, there were laws on the books, but no one bothered to enforce them. The employees were always tipped off if there was going to be an inspection. "Quick," they'd say, "into the boxes!" And we children would climb into the big boxes the finished shirts were stored in. Then some shirts were

The boy at the center of this picture of a garment sweatshop in 1889 was only 12 years old. More than 250,000 boys and girls under the age of 15 worked in factories and mines in 1900.

58

piled on top of us, and when the inspector came—no children. The factory always got an okay from the inspector, and I suppose someone at City Hall got a little something, too.

The employers didn't recognize anyone working for them as a human being. You were not allowed to sing. Operators would have liked to have sung.... We weren't allowed to talk to each other. Oh, no, they would sneak up behind if you were found talking to your next colleague. You were admonished: "If you keep on you'll be fired." If you went to the toilet and you were there longer than the floor lady thought you should be, you would be laid off for half a day and sent home. And, of course, that meant no pay. You were not allowed to have your lunch on the fire escape in the summertime. The door was locked to keep us in....

The employers had a sign in the elevator that said: "If you don't come in on Sunday, don't come in on Monday." You were expected to work every day if they need you and the pay was the same whether you worked extra or not....

If the season was over, we were told, "You're laid off. Shift for yourself." How did you live? After all, you didn't earn enough to save any money. Well, the butcher trusted you. He knew you'd pay him when you started work again. Your landlord, he couldn't do anything but wait, you know. Sometimes relatives helped out. There was no welfare, no pension, no unemployment insurance. There was nothing. We were much worse off than the poor are today because we had nothing to lean on; nothing to hope for except to hope that the shop would open again and that we'd have work.

Marie Ganz, who traveled with her mother to New York from Galicia in 1895, described working in a garment sweatshop.

We sat in long rows, our bodies bent over the machines, the work we turned out fell into wooden bins attached to the part of the machine facing us. No one girl made an entire garment. As each girl completed her part the garment was passed on to the next girl by Levinson [the foreman], who was always walking back and forth urging us on. Should a girl lag behind he would prod her, sometimes pulling on the garment to hurry it on to another worker.

"Hurry! Don't you see that the sleevemaker soon will have no work?" he would shout.

This sort of thing created a spirit of competition for self-preservation that ended only when the worker, too weak to compete longer with a stronger sister, broke down.

Before many days I discovered another phase of the speed-up system. At the end of each week the girl who had turned in the least work was dropped from the payroll. Knowledge of this fact had the effect of keeping the girls working like mad.

Around 1910, a woman brings garments home to be sewed. It was common for mothers to take their young children with them to the factories where they worked.

A woman making coats in a New York City sweatshop in 1909. The long hours took their toll: the death rate for young working women was twice that of those who did not work.

The children of this Jewish family made garters for a few cents apiece.

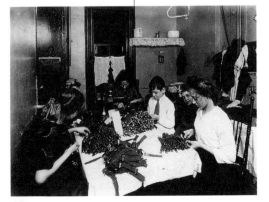

Emma Goldman found her first job in America in a garment factory, sewing "ulsters," or overcoats, 10.5 hours a day, 6 days a week, for $2.50 a week. Still, as she related, it was better than the factory where she had worked in Russia, though even here the foreman was brutal.

The amazing thing to me was that no one else in the factory seemed to be so affected as I, no one but my neighbor, frail little Tanya. She was delicate and pale, frequently complained of headaches, and often broke into tears when the task of handling heavy ulsters proved too much for her. One morning, as I looked up from my work, I discovered her all huddled in a heap. She had fallen in a faint. I called to the foreman to help me carry her to the dressing-room, but the deafening noise of the machines drowned my voice. Several girls nearby heard me and began to shout. They ceased working and rushed over to Tanya. The sudden stopping of the machines attracted the foreman's attention and he came over to us. Without even asking the reason for the commotion, he shouted: "Back to your machines! What do you mean stopping work now? Do you want to be fired? Get back at once!" When he spied the crumpled body of Tanya, he yelled: "What the hell is the matter with her?" "She has fainted," I replied, trying hard to control my voice. "Fainted, nothing," he sneered, "she's only shamming."

"You are a liar and a brute!" I cried, no longer able to keep back my indignation.

I bent over Tanya, loosened her waist, and squeezed the juice of an orange I had in my lunch basket into her half-opened mouth. Her face was white, a cold sweat on her forehead. She looked so ill that even the foreman realized she had not been shamming. He excused her for the day. "I will go with Tanya," I said; "you can deduct from my pay for the time." "You can go to hell, you wildcat!" he flung after me.

Harry Roskolenko, who immigrated with his family from eastern Europe at the beginning of the 20th century, had his first sight of a garment factory when he took an apple to his father who worked there. Roskolenko explained why the factories were called sweatshops.

When I arrived at the factory there he was, my father, soaking wet with sweat. It was just an ordinary shop, I discovered, with nothing special about the men, the work, the heat, the dirt, the pay, the boss, the production. It was a factory with a hundred workers stripped down to their pants. All sorts of tailoring, cutting, and pressing machines were whirling, whirring and steaming away. I was fascinated for a few minutes—then I saw my father. I lost the magic of a new place at once. The inventions were gone—and there was a man of 50, pressing a cloak with a 10-pound steam iron.

It was summer sweat, winter sweat, all sorts of sweat; bitter, sour, stinking, moldy—through all the seasons of the year. Not one fan to blow up some wind. The fans were in the boss's office.... A few pigeons would reach the fire escapes for the bits of stale bread that a worker had put there—for a moment of flight and magic. The pigeons would make off, when the steam blew their way. Instead of fans there were foremen walking about, fuming and blowing, their voices like dogs barking at other dogs....

Outside, the temperature was almost 100 degrees. Indoors, it rose to 110 or 120—humid, steamy, all-encasing, gluey. At the tables they got so much per garment pressed or so much for sewing on sleeves, collars, linings, bodies—whatever went to make up the finished garment. It was so little usually and the cause of many strikes and sudden stoppages. With this system of sweating, every worker gave up his lunchtime—the minutes saved, up to no time at all—and then back to the steam and the machines, and to the *gontser macher* [Yiddish for "big shot"] barking to his dogs.

A fire in the Triangle Shirtwaist Factory in New York on March 25, 1911, claimed the lives of 147 workers, mainly Jewish and Italian immigrant women and girls. Louis Waldman remembered the tragic day.

When we arrived at the scene, the police had thrown a cordon around the area and the firemen were help-lessly fighting the blaze. The eighth, ninth, and tenth stories of the building were now an enormous roaring cornice of flames.

Word had spread through the East Side, by some magic of terror, that the plant of the Triangle Waist Company was on fire and that several hundred workers were trapped. Horrified and helpless, the crowds—I among them—looked up at the burning building, saw girl after girl appear at the reddened windows, pause for a terrified moment, and then leap to the pavement below, to land as mangled, bloody pulp. This went on for what seemed a ghastly eternity. Occasionally a girl who had hesitated too long was licked by pursuing flames and, screaming with clothing and hair ablaze, plunged like a living torch to the street. Life nets held by the firemen were torn by the impact of the falling bodies....

One of the owners of the Triangle Waist Company who was in the building at the outbreak of the fire left it hurriedly without unlocking the exits, thus dooming the girls inside. Nor had the girls ever been permitted to use the passenger elevators, due to the owners' fear that they might carry out stolen mate-rial.

When the fire was over the toll of the Triangle disaster was 147 killed and burned to death and several hundred suffering from serious burns. Police and firemen on entering the charred building discovered bodies literally burned to the bone. Black-ened skeletons were found bending over machines. In one of the narrow elevator shafts of the building they found lifeless bodies piled six stories high.

A Jewish garment worker in New York City in 1920.

Men, too, worked in the garment factories, as in this shop in 1915. But employers preferred to hire women and children, who earned less money for the same hours of work.

THE UNION MOVEMENT

The shirtwaist makers, who sewed the long blouses that were popular in the early 20th century, staged the first large garment industry strike in the fall of 1909. Here, well-to-do women, who did not have to work for a living, came to show their support for the strikers.

The great influx of eastern European Jews after 1880 led to attempts to organize unions of Jewish workers. Bernard Weinstein, one of the organizers of the United Hebrew Trades, tells of a visit he made to a Jewish union.

Among the unions we had at the end of the 1890s a few were composed of old men, like the pressers', the butchers', the ragpickers' locals. One of these that we of the United Hebrew Trades helped organize in 1894 was a union of cleaners. Its members, who had mostly been tailors in Europe, operated out of cellars and worked by hand. They'd take dirty old clothes, wash them with benzene, dye them with brushes, and then press them. Many a time their pails of kerosene would spill over and cause fires in the tenements.

One day three of us from the United Hebrew Trades were invited to a meeting held on the top floor of a loft at 49 Henry Street.... When we arrived, everyone was sitting around a table facing the chairman; all wore yarmulkes except a few younger members with hats. Most were dressed in long smocks resembling caftans. Everyone had a glass of beer in hand, and before him a plate of herring and chunks of pumpernickel.

The place was half dark from the smoke of pipes and one could have been deafened by the banging of the beer glasses. A few fellows served as waiters and would steadily put down glasses of beer with a *"l'chaim"* [a toast in Hebrew: "to life"].

The chairman stood on a platform in the middle of the room. When he noticed us—we hadn't known where to sit among the hundred or so members—he summoned us to the head of the table. As we drew near, everyone rose and as the chairman recited our "pedigree" we were resoundingly toasted with the clinking of glasses....

Sidney Hillman, the taller man at center, was president of the Amalgamated Clothing Workers from 1914 until his death in 1946. Here, he and other workers celebrate their victory in a 1915 strike.

The noise grew. Someone began a Simchat Torah melody ["Rejoicing with the Torah," a festival honoring the Torah, which is celebrated with feasting and merrymaking]; glasses continually refilled from a nearby barrel; also pails of ice to keep the beer cold. Finally I asked my bearded neighbor: "What's the occasion?"

"How should I know?" he answered. "Every meeting is like this, or else we wouldn't show up. The men give a few dimes apiece, and we have a Simchat Torah. That's how we are—sometimes we kiss each other from happiness, sometimes we fight."

At the end of each of our speeches, we all cried out, "Long live the union!" as the old Jews applauded and bumped glasses. Meanwhile a few started to move aside the tables and began dancing to a Hasidic tune.

In our report to the UHT, we called this group the Simchat Torah Union.

Sadie Frowne immigrated to New York from Poland in the 1890s. She worked in sweatshops on Allen Street on the Lower East Side of Manhattan and in Brownsville, Brooklyn. When she was interviewed in 1902, she described the importance of the union.

We recently finished a strike in our business. It spread all over and the United Brotherhood of Garment Workers was in it. That takes in the cloakmakers, coatmakers, and all the others. We struck for shorter hours, and after being out four weeks won the fight. We only have to work nine and a half hours a day and we get the same pay as before. So the union does good after all in spite of what some people say against it—that it just takes our money and does nothing.

I pay 25 cents a month to the union, but I do not begrudge that because it is for our benefit. The next strike is going to be for a raise of wages, which we all ought to have. But though I belong to the Union I am not a Socialist or an Anarchist. I don't know exactly what those things mean. There is a little expense for charity, too. If any worker is injured or sick we all give money to help.

Women played an important role in organizing the unions. In 1905, Rose Schneiderman described her role in starting a garment workers' union.

We formed a committee composed of my friend Bessie Mannis, who worked with me, myself, and a third girl. Bravely we ventured into the office of the United Cloth Hat and Cap Makers Union and told the man in charge that we would like to be organized....

We were told that we would have to have at least 25 women from a number of factories before we could acquire a charter. Novices that we were, we used the simplest methods. We waited at the doors of factories and, as the girls were leav-

Garment industry strikers gather in 1913. Someone holds a sign in Yiddish.

A fire broke out inside the Triangle Shirtwaist Factory in New York City on March 25, 1911. Because the doors to the workrooms were locked, hundreds of workers were trapped inside. To escape, some young women leaped out of the windows to their death. More than 140 died, a disaster that led to reforms in the city and state labor codes.

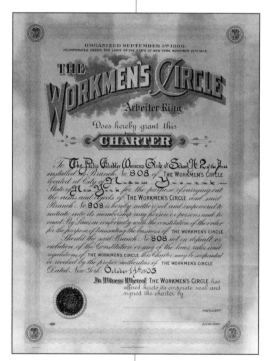

Founded in 1900, the Workmen's Circle (Arbeiter Ring) was a fraternal organization of Jewish laborers. It provided health insurance to members at a time when employers did not. Local chapters of the organization also sponsored cultural and educational activities.

ing for the day, we would approach them and speak our piece. We had blank pledges of membership ready in case some could be persuaded to join us. Within days we had the necessary number, and in January 1903 we were chartered as Local 23, and I was elected secretary.

It was such an exciting time. A new life opened for me. All of a sudden I was not lonely anymore. I had shop and executive board meetings to attend as well as the meetings of our unit.... The only cloud in the picture was mother's attitude toward my becoming a trade unionist. She kept saying I'd never get married because I was so busy—a prophecy which came true. Of course, what she resented most of all was my being out of the house almost every evening. But for me it was the beginning of a period that molded all my subsequent life and opened wide many doors that might have remained closed to me....

That June we decided to put our strength to the test. In the summer the men usually worked only half-day on Saturdays, which was pay day. But even when there was no work we women had to hang around until three or four o'clock before getting our pay. I headed a committee which informed Mr. Fox that we wanted to be paid at the same time as the men. Mr. Fox was a portly gentleman of German extraction, a rather handsome man with luminous brown eyes and a piercing look. After I presented our case he studied me with a grin and then said, "You want your pay, do you? Well, I'll see about it." He didn't say outright that he agreed; he wouldn't give us that much satisfaction. But on the first Saturday in July, when we went for our pay at twelve noon, there it was ready for us....

Our convention that year, 1903, opened as usual on the first of May, always regarded as a kind of international workers' holiday. We took the day off on our own, receiving no pay. I was elected delegate from my union. We women rode in the parade in a wagon, for it was not considered ladylike to participate on foot. It was an exciting and heartwarming day and I enjoyed it tremendously.

In 1904, Sam Schaeffer, who had been branded a "scab" after he had worked during a strike, sent the following appeal to the Pants Makers Union in Boston. Schaeffer now begged to be accepted as a union member.

Dear brothers, I beg you to have mercy on my children. If you would come in my house you would see how frozen my stove is, and how my children shiver terribly with cold—on empty little stomachs—just as I do. But I can only answer my dear little children with a sigh: "I was a scab, therefore we must starve from hunger and cold." I cannot justify myself against the union. I can do nothing.

Dear brothers, I hope that among you will be found men with feeling. I know that among you there are fathers who know that children ask for bread: How does it feel when you have nothing to give them?

Dear brothers, I will ask you something, but answer me feelingly. Are my children responsible for my being a scab? Are they to be blamed because their father is a tomfool? Answer me, are they to be blamed? I beg of you in the name of my little ones let me in the union; we are cold, we are hungry, you are men, have sympathy, have mercy, brothers. I am no scab, I am to be blamed, I committed a crime, I did take money from the union, all is true. I can no longer give it back, I will do it no more.

Brothers, men, men, brothers, we are hungry, we are cold, take me in the union, let me go to work. Brothers, if you do not take me in the union, let me go to work. Brothers, if you do not take me in the union the blame will be upon you. I am doing my duty. I beg and keep begging you to take me in the union.

Louis Waldman worked as a cutter in the garment industry, although later he became a lawyer. In his autobiography he remembered taking part in the great cloak makers' strike of 1910.

Without hesitation I walked out with the rest of the workers, and, since I was now on strike, I joined the union. Our grievances were many and just and included an upward revision of the wage scale, the shortening of the work day, and improvement of sanitary conditions, and called for an investigation into possible fire hazards as well as demands for the abolition of the sweatshop system. More than fifty thousand cloakmakers answered the strike call....

On the second day of the strike, as we approached our factory, we found several toughs strolling nonchalantly back and forth before the entrance. The older and more experienced workers looked at each other and whispered: "Shtarke!" I had heard the expression before. These "shtarker" were in reality strong-arm men, gangsters, hired by the employers to help break the strike. As we proceeded to march up and down before the building, not only peacefully but timidly as well, the strong-arm men soon began to walk at our sides pretending to be ordinary pedestrians. Now and then one would brutally push a picket off the sidewalk, sending him flying into the gutter, at the same time muttering to the stunned picket: "Quit pushing!" If the picket stood firm the gangster would then, in "self-defense," knock him down.

All day long this brutal game went on, but the pickets stuck it out. And the police, I observed, were nowhere to be seen while the thugs were at work. This state of affairs called for the special attention of the cutters. They were the most Americanized group in the union, while the tailors had the customary timidity of immigrants, fearful to strike out in defense of their rights. The cutters were thus obliged to act as an emergency squad, subject to the call of the tailors wherever the going was toughest. They pitted their courage and bare hands against the blackjacks and lead pipes of the gangsters.

Samuel Gompers

Samuel Gompers took his first job at the age of 10. As an apprentice to a shoemaker in London, England, where he was born in 1850, Gompers earned six pennies a week. At night, he went to a religious school where he studied Hebrew and the Torah.

When Gompers was 13, his family emigrated to the United States. He and his father began to make cigars in their tenement apartment on New York City's Lower East Side. Ten years later, while working in a cigar factory, Gompers joined a union and soon was elected president of the local chapter. He led his first strike in 1877, in protest against unsanitary working conditions. The factory owner granted the workers' demands.

At that time, the leading American labor organization was the Knights of Labor. Its leader, Terence V. Powderly, wanted to build a national union that would accept skilled and unskilled workers in all occupations. However, the Knights were unjustly blamed for the bloody Haymarket Riot in Chicago in 1886, and the organization lost the support of many members.

In that same year, Gompers helped to form an association of unions of skilled workers, such as carpenters, plumbers, and machinists. He was elected the first president of the American Federation of Labor (AFL) and served in that post, with the exception of one year, until his death in 1924.

Gompers had clearly defined goals for the AFL: he wanted to win acceptance of an eight-hour workday as well as better wages and working conditions. When more radical labor organizations appeared, the AFL seemed moderate by comparison. Gompers was then able to win support for his demands from Congress and business leaders. Through his leadership, the organized labor movement secured a permanent role in American society.

Julius Meyer (upper left) was a merchant who traded with Native Americans in the 1860s. Because he knew several Native American languages, he also served as an interpreter.

PIONEERS IN THE WEST

Jews were living in Texas when it was still part of Mexico. Moses Albert Levy, a doctor who joined Sam Houston's army during the revolution against the Mexican government in 1835, took part in the battle in which the Texans captured San Antonio from the Mexicans. Levy wrote to his sister in the eastern United States, describing his role.

When we reached the American camp after suffering a thousand deaths in traveling through and sleeping in the cold bleak prairies night after night without a tree or shrub to shelter us from the cold rain and wind, we found the greatest state of confusion and dissatisfaction. The men had left their families and homes with a view to driving the enemy out of their country at once, and then returning home.... [But the commander decided to starve out the Mexican army that occupied San Antonio] and prevented the Americans from immediately storming the place.... Finally affairs became so bad that the army broke up in confusion.... We would all have been cut by the enemy when I, *insignificant I,* and another individual [asked for] volunteers who would join us two in storming the town and fort that very night.... I harangued them for a few minutes and thus succeeded in getting 300 men. We laid our plans, appointed our leaders, and about daylight marched up to the enemy's halls, got into some strong houses in town and after a regular storm of five days and nights...during the whole of which the enemy kept up an incessant firing, we forced them to surrender.... Our men fought like devils, (even I fought). I worked in the ditches, I dressed the sick and wounded, I cheered the men.... For five days and nights I did not sleep that many hours, running about without

The Rose Brothers Trading Post in Alaska around 1888.

a coat or hat, dirty and ragged, but thank God escaped uninjured.... I have crossed a street when more than 200 muskets were shot at me, our men begging me not to expose myself as I was a double man, being both soldier and surgeon.

Jewish traders were often the first European settlers on the western frontier. Frequently, they acted as links between the Native Americans and settlers. In the 1840s, Augusta Levy and her husband, Meyer, came from Germany and settled in what is today Minnesota. Meyer Levy offered to let a group of Native American chiefs use his home for a council meeting. Unfortunately, he did not inform his wife. Augusta wrote about the incident in her memoirs.

Next day about eleven o'clock, a beautiful, bright day, we could see a great way up and down the river; all at once we saw the greatest sight I ever saw. About 50 canoes appeared, filled with all the Indian chiefs, all of them dressed and painted, and with big bunches of feathers on their heads and tomahawks in their hands. They were dressed in their best, and glistened as if a procession all shining with gold and silver was coming down the river.

I didn't know anything about their arrangements, so little Willie [her son] and I were scared.... I ran to shut all the windows and lock all the doors. We were alone in the house. Then we hid ourselves in the dark room....

They knocked and knocked but I would not open the door. Then I heard someone pounding and pounding, and kicking against the door. This noise was not by moccasins but by boots. Then someone tried to break in the door. Then I heard swearing, in English and German, but I wouldn't open the door. Finally my husband came around to the kitchen window and called my name. Then of course I thought I was all right, and quickly came out of my corner. I asked him if he didn't see the Indians around by the front door. They were all there, with their tomahawks, to kill us. He said, "Open the doors quickly, in Heaven's name! What did you lock yourself in for?" Said I, "Didn't you see the Indians at the front door to kill us?" Said he, "If you don't open the doors, quick, I'll kick them in!" So I opened the kitchen door to let him in and he went to the front door at once to let the Indians in, while I hastened back to my hiding place.

If there was any scalping to be done, I thought they could take him first. But they all went very quietly into the dining room, sat down on the floor, had a smoke all around, and then they asked for some water. My husband called me to bring in a pail of water and a pint cup, that he would stay in sight.... After this I got up courage enough, as I didn't see any scalping done, to peep in....

My husband saw I was excited so he took me into the other room and told me to have patience.... They took a smoke all around again and then shook hands and departed. I wished them a pleasant journey, and never to return.

As Others Saw Them

The Polish writer Henry Sienkiewicz toured the West in 1877. He noted:

At the recently discovered gold mines where adventurers quickly congregate, where the knife, the revolver, and the terrifying lynch law still prevail, where an American merchant hesitates to open shop out of fear both for his merchandise and his life, the first stores are generally established by Jews. By their courtesy, kind words, and, above all, extension of credit, they win the favor of the most dangerous adventurers.... And once having the revolvers of the desperadoes on their side, the storekeepers conduct their affairs with complete safety.... I saw our [Polish] Jews operating stores under [these] conditions...at Deadwood, Dakota; Darwin, California; and Virginia City, Nevada.

One of the three Oppenheimer brothers who arrived in Oregon in 1857. Although this is a studio photograph, he poses with a pistol and knife under his belt. One brother, Marcus Oppenheimer, later founded the town of Marcus in Washington State.

Max Stein, a mounted policeman in Pueblo, Colorado, around 1900.

Jewish homesteaders near Helena, Montana, around 1890. The man holding the cup, just behind the young girl, is Rabbi Samuel Schulman.

Morris Schloss left his birthplace in Russia in 1842, when he was 14. He lived for six years in England and then came to the United States. A year later, the gold rush took him to California, with a peddler's wagon in a wooden crate. Almost at once, Schloss learned that the price of goods in California bore no relation to what they were worth elsewhere.

I arrived in San Francisco, September 25, 1849, landing at the foot of Broadway Street with my baggage. I brought with me a wagon packed in a large box and, at the landing, a man asked me what was in the box. I told him, a wagon, and he asked the price of it. I answered $125, and he offered me $100, which rather surprised me, as the man had not seen the contents of the box. I accepted his offer, and he paid me in gold dust. I had only paid $15 for this wagon in New York, so I thought this was rather a good beginning for me.

The man was very careful in opening the box not to break the lid, and then, taking out the wagon, he said to me: "Stranger, you may keep the wagon, for I only want the box" (for which I had paid $3). "That case is what I want" he said. "I am a cobbler, and in the daytime it will be my shop, and at night, my residence." That box measured seven feet by four feet.

Solomon Nunez Carvalho, born in Charleston, South Carolina, in 1815, became a painter and photographer. Explorer John Charles Frémont invited Carvalho to accompany his western expedition across the Rocky Mountains in 1853. Carvalho's photographs of the journey have been lost, but his written account survives.

The crossing of the Grand River, the eastern fork of the Colorado, was attended with much difficulty and more danger. The weather was exceedingly cold, the ice on the margin of either side of the river was over 18 inches thick; the force of the stream always kept the passage in the centre open; the distance between the ice, was at our crossing, about 200 yards.... The animals could scarcely keep their footing on the ice, although the men had been engaged for half an hour in strewing it with sand. The river was about six feet deep, making it necessary to swim our animals across....

I think I must have been in the water, at least a quarter of an hour. The awful plunge from the ice into the water, I never shall have the ambition to try again; the weight of my body on the horse, naturally made him go under head and all; I held on as fast as a cabin boy to a main-stay in a gale of wind. If I had lost my balance it is most probable I should have drowned. I was nearly drowned as it was, and my clothes froze stiff upon me when I came out of it....

It is most singular, that with all the exposure that I was subjected to on this journey, I never took the slightest cold, either in my head or on my chest; I do not recollect ever sneezing. While at home, I ever was most susceptible to cold.

Solomon Floerscheim came to the United States from Germany in 1879. He soon went west to New Mexico. In 1881, while working in Las Vegas, New Mexico, he met the famous outlaw Billy the Kid. His son Carl wrote:

On July 12, 1881, my father...traveled until dusk until he finally noticed a light in the distance. He drove toward a light shining in a window and he knocked on the door. He was told, "Come in." To my father's surprise, the room was used as a saloon. The only person in this room was a young man about my father's age. My father asked "What road do you take to the nearest ranch? Where is there a good place to eat and to get a room?" The man in the room told him of two places. On turning to go out, the stranger asked, "Do you want a drink of whiskey." "No," was the answer. Immediately, the young man drew a pistol and pointed it at my father. "Drink!"—and drink he did. "Where are you from; what's your name; what do you have with you; what are you doing here? Take another drink!"

Of course my father did not know until then that he was facing the Kid.... My father started to chide the outlaw. He even offered to trade guns with him. Billy preferred the pistol that had killed 21 men. It had a notch on the wood handle for every one killed. My father even had the nerve to ask Billy to come and see him when he came to Las Vegas—but he never really wanted to see him again.

My father did not remain in Fort Sumner that night.... He drove all night toward the ranch he was to visit and about 5 a.m. he arrived at his destination. It was the home of Sheriff Pat Garrett and his family.... After a good breakfast and a few hours rest, Garrett said to my father, "Sol, let's go back to Fort Sumner and get Billy." My father told him, "I've seen all that I want of that fellow. If you want him, you go and get him."

[That very day Sheriff Pat Garrett shot Billy the Kid.]

Sarah Thal and her husband were homesteaders in the Dakotas.

We had only one near neighbor, the Seligers, another Jewish family. Their cabin was so poorly built that during our first real blizzard they were afraid to spend the night there. Mr. Seliger came to our place and asked if he might have the team [of horses] to bring his wife and baby, but the storm was such that a team couldn't have found its way.

My husband advised him to keep to the plowed ground which ran from his door to ours. He returned home and late that night came to our place almost frozen. He had let go of his wife and baby for just a bit and had been searching for them since mid-afternoon.

The storm lasted three days. When it cleared mother and baby were found about 50 feet from their house frozen to death.... We heated water and thawed the bodies sufficient to fit in a home-made coffin. I remember that beautiful baby to this day. The frost glistened on her cheeks making her look like a wax doll.

The Hebrew Immigrant Aid Society attempted to settle Jewish immigrants in agricultural "colonies" in several western states. This picture shows some members of the 13 families who arrived at Cotopaxi, Colorado, in 1882.

The Barrie Levington family in front of their sod house near Anselmo, Nebraska, in 1888. On the plains where trees were scarce, settlers used chunks of sod as building blocks for their homes.

ANTI-SEMITISM

Social restrictions against Jews were sometimes proclaimed openly, as on this sign in front of a 1940s-style motel.

During the 1880s, upper-class Americans began to exclude prosperous Jews from their clubs, resorts, and social organizations. Nina Morais, descended from an old Sephardic Jewish family in Philadelphia, wrote in 1881:

In the popular mind the Jew is never judged as an individual, but as a specimen of a whole race whose members are identically of the same kind. [Non-Jews find the Jew] an objectionable character, whose shrewdness and questionable dealings in trade enable him to wear large diamonds and flashy clothes. He raises his voice beyond the fashionable key, in a language execrable to the ears of the English-speaking people. For the proprieties and amenities of cultured life he has no regard. His conversation rings upon the key-note of the dollar; his literature is the quotations of the market. Mean in pence, he spends his pounds with an ostentation that shocks people. Of the higher sympathies he has none; the finer feelings he cannot appreciate. In a word, he is foreign—outlandish—a Jew.

Anti-Semitism increased with the arrival of larger numbers of Jews from eastern Europe after 1880. Mary Sydney Ostrow told an interviewer about discrimination in Providence, Rhode Island.

Before my Uncle William was to bring his bride from New York to Providence he went with my father to look at an apartment. My father had a rather long beard, but it was a nice-sized beard. They went to look at empty apartments. At that time, if anyone had an empty apartment, there was a sign in the window, "For Rent." They went to Orms Street just above Douglas Avenue.... There were two nice houses, and my uncle rang the doorbell. The woman who answered, gave one look at them, spat, and said, "Jews" and slammed the door in their face. So you see, the Jews did not live in that area, for no one would rent them a place. That was about the year 1892.

Edna Ferber, who would become a Pulitzer Prize–winning novelist, grew up in the town of Ottumwa, Iowa, during the 1890s. She recalled:

On Saturdays and on unusually busy days when my father could not take the noon dinner, it became my duty to take his midday meal down to him.... This little trip from the house on Wapello Street to the store on Main Street amounted to running the gauntlet. I didn't mind so much the Morey girl. She sat in front of her house perched on the white gatepost, waiting, a child about my age, with long, red curls, a freckled face, very light green eyes. She swung her long legs, idly. At sight of me her listlessness fled.

"Hello, sheeny!" [This is a derogatory slang word.] Then variations on this. This, one learned to receive equably. Besides, the natural retort to her baiting was to shout, airily, "Red Head! Wet the bed!"

But as I approached the Main Street corner there sat a row of vultures perched on the iron railing at the side of Sargent's drugstore. These were not children, they were men. Perhaps to me, a small child, they seemed older than they were, but their ages must have ranged from 18 to 30. There they sat, perched on the black iron rail, their heels hooked behind the lower rung. They talked almost not at all.... Vacant-eyed, they stared and spat and sat humped and round-shouldered, doing nothing, thinking nothing, being nothing. Suddenly their lackluster eyes brightened, they shifted, they licked their lips and spat with more relish. From afar they had glimpsed their victim, a plump little girl in a clean gingham frock, her black curls confined by a ribbon bow.

Every fiber of me shrieked to run the other way. My eyes felt hot and wide. My face became scarlet. I must walk carefully so as not to spill the good hot dinner. Now then. Now.

"Sheeny! Has du gesak de Isaac! De Moses! De Levi! Heh, sheeny, what you got!" Good Old Testament names. They doubtless heard them in their Sunday worship, but did not make the connection, quite. They then brought their hands, palms up, above the level of their shoulders and wagging them back and forth, "Oy-you sheeny! Run! Go on, run!"

I didn't run. I glared.

In the 20th century, Jews have been among the targets of the Ku Klux Klan, particularly in western states.

The Leo Frank Lynching

In 1913, Leo Frank was accused of murdering a 13-year-old girl who worked in his pencil factory in Atlanta, Georgia. His trial was held in an atmosphere of anti-Semitic violence, as a reporter for the *New York Herald Tribune* wrote: "Mobs choked the area around the courthouse. Men with rifles stood at the open windows, some aimed at the jury, some aimed at the judge. Over and over, louder and louder the men repeated the chant: 'Hang the Jew, Hang the Jew.'... The mobs kept up their chant. I can still hear them screaming...through the open windows. And inside the courtroom, spectators were allowed to give free vent to their anti-Semitism. The jury was threatened with death unless it brought in a verdict of guilty. The judge was threatened with death if he didn't pass a sentence of hanging. No deputies tried to clear the windows of the courtroom."

On the testimony of a janitor who worked in the factory, Frank was convicted and sentenced to death. Because the evidence against him was so flimsy, the governor of the state commuted the sentence to life imprisonment in June 1915. Two months later, a mob kidnapped Frank from a prison farm and lynched him near a place called Five Points.

Clarence Feibelman, who, like Frank, was of German Jewish descent, told an interviewer years later: "We knew Leo Frank. We knew his wife and her family very well. Of course, the charges were ridiculous, as far as I was concerned. He couldn't be guilty of such a thing.

"I happened to be at Five Points the morning after Frank was lynched. There must have been five or six of these men, they would be called red-necks, drove into Five Points. And they displayed a piece of the rope with which they had lynched Frank. They were pretty well received by the folks at Five Points. You can imagine how I felt. They were hazardous times. They were frightening times. We were all frightened."

Anti-Semitism made it difficult for Jews in workplaces where there were few other Jews. In 1907 a reader wrote a letter to the Jewish Daily Forward, *a New York Yiddish newspaper that played an important role in the lives of eastern European Jewish immigrants.*

Worthy Editor,

I am 18 years old and a machinist by trade. During the past year I suffered a great deal, just because I am a Jew. It is common knowledge that my trade is run mainly by the Gentiles, and, working among the Gentiles, I have seen things that cast a dark shadow on the American labor scene. Just listen:

I worked in a shop in a small town of New Jersey, with twenty Gentiles. There was one other Jew besides me, and both of us endured the greatest hardships. That we were insulted goes without saying. At times we were even beaten up. We work in an area where there are many factories, and once, when we were leaving the shop, a group of workers fell on us like hoodlums and beat us. To top it off, we and one of our attackers were arrested. The hoodlum was let out on bail, but we, beaten and bleeding, had to stay in jail. At the trial, they fined the hoodlum eight dollars and let him go free.

After that I went to work on a job in Brooklyn. As soon as they found out that I was a Jew they began to torment me so that I had to leave the place. I have already worked at many places, and I either have to leave, voluntarily, or they fire me because I am a Jew.

Till now, I was alone and didn't care. At this trade you can make good wages, and I had enough. But now I've brought my parents over, and of course I have to support them.

Lately I've been working on one job for three months and I would be satisfied, but the worm of anti-Semitism is beginning to eat at my bones again. I go to work in the mornings as to Gehenna [hell], and I run away at night as from a fire. It's impossible to talk to them because they are common boors, so-called "American sports." I have already tried in various ways, but the only way to deal with them is with a strong fist. But I am too weak and they are too many.

Perhaps you can help me in this matter. I know it is not an easy problem.

In 1911, Louis Geffen moved to Atlanta, where his father Tobias became the rabbi in the Shearith Israel synagogue. Geffen's family was among the Jews who came from eastern Europe at the end of the 19th and beginning of the 20th century. He remembered the prejudice.

Many of them spoke the English language with an accent. Most of them spoke Yiddish fluently. When my father would walk down the street sometimes, since he was a man with a beard, which was unusual in those days, and he also wore the type of long coat that the rabbis of the old country would wear, he would sometimes hear insinuating remarks. "Say, there goes that Jew," and smirks and jeers, or something of that nature.

Arthur Goldberg, who would one day be a justice of the U.S. Supreme Court, grew up in Chicago, where he had been born in 1908.

Anti-Semitism? That we knew. Crawford Avenue, when we lived on Lawndale, was the demarcation point between us and the Poles. And as a kid, all the anti-Semitism of the old country carried over. I remember as a kid there were fights and I was an ammunition bearer—that's a fact. I passed bricks to my brothers. If the Poles invaded our area, it was defended by throwing bricks, and as a kid six or seven years old, my job was to pass out bricks, and my brothers stood on the roofs and threw them at the Polish kids. I didn't know what the hell got into me—all the Jewish kids went to a mostly Jewish high school. I didn't. I went to a high school where the Jews were in a minority and Polish and Czechoslovene kids were a majority. Had to fight my way home every day. Yes. Every day. It sounds like an exaggeration, but the Polish kids would lie around and when Jewish kids would want to walk home—there were some—we had to fight our way home....

[Being a Jew influenced Goldberg's choice of a career.] Jews, who place a great premium on justice, found their horizons were very limited. How many Jews were in the newspaper industry? Not many. Jews didn't know investment banking; couldn't get a job in a bank. Executive suites were closed to them. The garment industry was open to you if you had some money. We had none. Where the hell could Jews go? Somehow you could get a job in a law office or hang out your shingle.

As Others Saw Them

The Reverend A. E. Patton, a Protestant minister, visited Ellis Island in 1912 and wrote:

For a real American to visit Ellis Island, and there look upon the Jewish hordes, ignorant of all true patriotism, filthy, vermin-infested, stealthy and furtive in manner, too lazy to enter into real labor, too cowardly to face frontier life, too lazy to work as every American farmer has to work, too filthy to adopt ideals of cleanliness from the start, too bigoted to surrender any racial traditions or to absorb any true Americanism, for a real American to see those items of a filthy, greedy, never patriotic stream flowing in to pollute all that has made America good as she is—is to awaken in his thoughtful mind desires to check and lessen this source of pollution.

In recent years, White Power groups have adopted the Nazi swastika as a symbol of their hate-based movement. Here, anti-Semitic slogans were scrawled on the walls of a Jewish community center.

Carl and Laura Adler with their children, Theresa and Leo, in Baker, Oregon, around 1897.

CHAPTER FIVE

PUTTING DOWN ROOTS

The formation of a religious congregation was the event that marked the establishment of a Jewish American community. The 17th-century Jews of New Amsterdam gathered for prayers each Saturday (the Sabbath) in the house of one of the settlers and soon purchased a plot of land for a cemetery. Not until the festival of Passover in 1730 was the first American synagogue dedicated, in New York City. Colonial congregations were led in prayer by a hazan (cantor).

In colonial times, Jewish Americans took an active role in their communities, contributing to charities and serving as public officials. Children of well-to-do Jews attended private schools with Christians, and a sizable number married gentiles (non-Jews), causing concern that the Jewish tradition in America would disappear. In 1820, Jacob Lyons of Savannah, Georgia, sorrowfully predicted that "a synagogue...will not be found in the United States fifty years hence."

Ten years later, however, the wave of Ashkenazi German Jews began to arrive, and they would revitalize American Judaism. The Ashkenazi newcomers established their own synagogues, for they were uncomfortable with the

Sephardic rituals of the older, established congregations. The German Jews brought the first rabbis (a Hebrew word meaning "teacher") to the United States. In Europe the rabbis' traditional role was to interpret religious law; congregations hired them to serve in that capacity. In practice, however, rabbis in the United States were called on to perform the duties of the hazan and became religious leaders as well as teachers.

Many of the German rabbis who came to the United States introduced a new trend in European Jewish religious thought. This movement, which became known as Reform Judaism, modified certain traditional practices in an effort to adapt to modern circumstances. For example, in Reform congregations men and women sat together instead of separately; sermons and some prayers were in English instead of Hebrew; and men discarded such traditional marks of piety as the yarmulke (skullcap) and the tallith, or prayer shawl. Many Reform Jews also abandoned the rules of kosher food preparation.

Isaac M. Wise, a Bohemian-born rabbi, was among the most important leaders of Reform Judaism in the United States. While serving the B'nai Jeshurun congregation in Cincinnati, Wise established the Union of American

Hebrew Congregations (UAHC) in 1873 to unite Reform Jewish leaders. Two years later, the UAHC founded Hebrew Union College in Cincinnati as a training school for Reform rabbis.

Other Jewish Americans felt that the Reform rabbis had abandoned too much of traditional Judaism. The first German rabbi in the United States, Abraham Rice, became a leading exponent of the Orthodox, or traditional, form of Judaism. In the 1840s, other American rabbis formed a third major branch of the religion, later known as Conservative Judaism, which attempted to forge a compromise between Orthodox and Reform practices. This three-way division in American Judaism has continued to the present day.

The Ashkenazi German Jews also made their influence felt in other ways. By sheer numbers they came to dominate the Jewish American community, and many of them quickly rose from peddlers to wealthy business leaders. A few German Jews built mansions on New York's fashionable Fifth Avenue—side by side with the homes of New York's non-Jewish elite. Less prosperous Jews congregated in neighborhoods where other immigrant groups, including the non-Jewish Germans, also lived.

The German Jews founded the first Jewish orphanages, hospitals, schools for Jewish children, and homes for the elderly. United Hebrew Charities, which had branches in many cities by the 1870s, attracted the support of all Jewish Americans in its work to assist fellow Jews in need.

Many other Jewish organizations arose in the 19th century to provide fellowship and support for their members. Most were *landsmanshaften,* associations of people who had come from the same town or region in Europe. In 1843, a group of German Jews in New York City organized the Independent Order of B'nai B'rith (Sons of the Covenant). It became the first national Jewish fraternal organization, raising money to provide aid for the needy. B'nai B'rith also established the Anti-Defamation League in 1913. Local Young Men's Hebrew Associations (YMHA), founded in the 1870s, provided recreational and educational services for Jewish youth.

After the arrival of Russian Jews, the Lower East Side of Manhattan became the largest and best-known Jewish section of any American city. By 1910, about one-fourth of all the people in Manhattan lived in this small area covering about 1.5 square miles. In the early 20th century, the signs on every shop were in Yiddish, the common language of the newcomers. Street peddlers hawked their wares from carts or stands. Cafes and delicatessens served food that brought memories of the old country. Kosher butchers sold meat that had been slaughtered under a rabbi's supervision. Public bathhouses, which offered showers and steam baths, were popular because the cramped tenements usually had only one sink and toilet for each floor. People thronged the streets late into the night, avoiding the gloomy apartments that offered little more than a place to sleep.

Yiddish-language newspapers such as the *Jewish Daily Forward* featured pages of letters in which the newcomers exchanged complaints and advice. Popular Yiddish

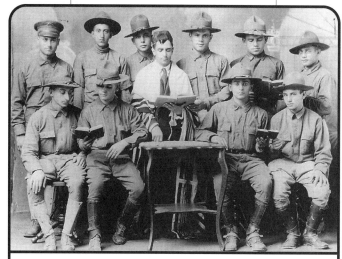

Jewish soldiers at Fort Riley, Kansas, with the rabbi-chaplain of the post in 1917.

theaters offered an endless variety of entertainment—plays, music, dancers, acrobats, and comedians.

Eastern European Jewish immigrants founded their own *landsmanshaften,* which offered their members insurance and interest-free loans and provided aid to the sick and elderly. The Workmen's Circle, founded in 1900, was an organization of laborers that offered help to those who were unemployed or unable to work. It rapidly grew to become one of the largest Jewish American organizations.

Eastern European Jews eagerly embraced the educational opportunities in their new country. The Educational Alliance, founded in 1893, offered classes in English, hygiene, home economics, art, music, gymnastics, and literature. Night classes in the immigrant neighborhoods were crowded with people who wanted to better themselves. There were also yeshivas, or religious schools, where young boys practiced reading the Hebrew prayers and studied the Torah. Girls usually received religious training from their mothers. Unlike the German Ashkenazim, virtually all of the eastern European Jews followed a strict, Orthodox form of Judaism.

At sundown on Friday, when the Sabbath begins, the shops of Jewish American neighborhoods closed. In traditional Jewish households, the men go to the synagogue for Sabbath evening service, while at home mothers prepare for the Sabbath dinner. Because cooking is forbidden on the Sabbath, meals are cooked before sundown. Two loaves of challah, or braided, yeasty bread, are baked and covered with a cloth until they are blessed. As the mother of the family recites a blessing, she lights candles to illuminate the house during the Sabbath.

At the evening meal, the father raises a cup of wine and recites the kiddush, a blessing of thanks to God for providing a day of rest. Such ceremonies, in which all members of the family are present, encourage a strong Jewish family life. Many of the holidays of the

Jewish year also involve family observances.

The Jewish year starts in the autumn with the holiday of Rosh Hashanah, which begins a 10-day period of repentance and meditation that ends on Yom Kippur, the Day of Atonement. Jews refer to Rosh Hashanah and Yom Kippur as the High Holy Days. The entire period is known as the Ten Days of Penitence. During this time, observant Jews ask forgiveness of others that they may have wronged during the past year.

On the fifth day after Yom Kippur, Sukkoth, or the Feast of Tabernacles, begins. It is a week-long feast of thanksgiving for the harvest. Observant Jewish families build Sukkoth booths, or huts, in the yards of their homes or synagogue. These booths are reminders of the dwellings in which the Israelites lived while wandering in the Sinai Desert. It is customary to eat a meal within the booths, which are often decorated with fruit and flowers by the children.

The day after the seventh day of Sukkoth is Shemini Atzereth (the Eighth Day of Conclusion), when prayers are said for a good harvest. The following day is Simchas Torah (Rejoicing with the Torah), when the yearly cycle of the reading of the Torah from the synagogue scroll is completed and then is immediately begun again.

On the 25th day of the month of Kislev in the Jewish calendar, Jews observe the eight days of Hanukkah (Dedication). It celebrates the Jews' victory over the Seleucid king in 165 B.C.E., when the Temple in Jerusalem was re-dedicated. Hanukkah is also known as the Feast of Lights because in Jewish homes candles are lit on each night of the festival: one candle on the first night, two on the following night, and so on. According to the Talmud, when Jewish warriors entered the Temple, they found only one flask of oil—enough to light the menorah (the seven-branched candlestick that is a symbol of Judaism) for just one day. Miraculously, however, the oil lasted for eight days.

Purim, or the Feast of Lots, is celebrated in February or March. It commemorates the victory of the Persian Jews over Haman, the king's adviser who plotted to destroy them. The story, told in the Book of Esther, relates that Haman cast lots to determine when he should send his forces against the Jews. The day he chose, the 13th of the month of Adar in the Jewish calendar, is a day when observant Jews fast. Esther, the Jewish wife of the Persian king, foiled his plans.

Thus, the 14th of Adar is a day of rejoicing.

In spring comes the feast of Pesach, or Passover, which commemorates the night when God passed over the homes of the Israelites while punishing the Egyptians. Though Passover is a week-long festival, the most important ceremony takes place in Jewish homes on the first night. This is the Seder, or dinner, when the youngest person at the table asks, as part of the ritual, "Why is this night different from all other nights?" and other questions that prompt a retelling of the story of the Jews' deliverance from slavery in Egypt. The meal itself is a reminder of that event. Four cups of wine are consumed, in thanksgiving for the four promises that God made to his chosen people. Matzo, or unleavened bread, is served because that was what the Jewish families baked in haste—they did not have time to let the bread rise—before their departure from Egypt. *Maror,* or bitter herbs, are eaten as a reminder of the bitterness of slavery; they are dipped into *haroset,* a mixture of apples, nuts, and wine that recalls the mortar the Jews were forced to make in building the pharaoh's city.

Jewish Americans have been strengthened by their close ties to family and community and the values of their religion. Traditional Jewish values—respect for education, hard work, thrift, concern for social justice, and religious devotion are among the reasons why so many sons and daughters of Jewish immigrants have become successful in the United States.

At a Passover seder in 1951, a seven-year-old boy asks the traditional four questions at a Jewish home for the elderly.

Hester Street on the Lower East Side of New York City, shown here around 1900, was the shopping area for the largest Jewish community in the United States.

A Sunday morning in the 1890s on Maxwell Street in Chicago, another center of urban Jewish American life.

THE NEIGHBORHOOD

Leopold Mayer arrived in Chicago to join two older brothers in 1850. Fifty years later he remembered what the city had been like.

Among the Jews themselves social entertainments gradually increased in number as the number of young men and women grew. Engagements were still few, but the young folks longed for diversion. In summer, carriage rides and joint walks in the fields, and in winter, sleigh-rides were in order; sometimes there were even theatre parties given.

The visiting day was Sunday, and it was always prearranged at whose house the following Sunday should be spent. There were no whist nor poker parties—as yet, the ladies did not play cards. Dances, today called balls, were difficult to arrange, but we had them....

The Jews in Chicago were fairly well situated.... Some had dry goods, others clothing stores; many were engaged in the cigar and tobacco business, and there were already a plumber and joiner, and even a carpenter here. Some—loading their goods upon a wagon, others upon their shoulders—followed the honorable vocation of peddling.

The houses in which we lived in those days in Chicago were modest one- or two-story frame dwellings.... The dietary laws were strictly observed and the Sabbath and festivals were celebrated with Jewish rites. Business houses were at no great distance from the homes and the men were generally to be found with their families after business hours. The women occupied themselves with needlework, to honor and obey their parents.... If the Jewish home was not quite what it was in Germany, it was still founded on filial love and respect.

Emily Fechheimer Seasongood wrote down her memories of growing up in Cincinnati, Ohio, during the 1870s. Many Germans, both Jewish and gentile, lived in the neighborhood that was called "Over the Rhine" because it was separated from the rest of the city by a canal.

Many Jewish people lived in this vicinity; some were very uneducated but very kindhearted. In the summer, one could see the male portion of the different families tilt their chairs across the gutter of the pavement in front of their homes and sit there in their shirt sleeves, with large palm fans in their hands. As not many people took vacations and few summer resorts were in vogue then, they took this method of trying to keep cool, as the summers were usually very warm....

I remember distinctly when the first streetcar ran. It was a wonderful event, was pulled by one horse, and all the children would run after it, and before its coming along would place pennies on the tracks to flatten, which were kept as souvenirs of the time.

[My cousin Henry] used to spend the day [at my house], and when it was time for him to go home, my dear mother had to remind him of the fact. As it was usually dusk at the time of his leaving, he would wait outside until he saw a lady and gentleman, so he could walk with them, as he was afraid to go alone. It was rumored about town that there was a man called Toe-smasher, who would run after people and smash their toes with an iron rod, which Henry probably thought of, and besides, there were many kidnappers. There were town criers in those days also, and many children were found by them and restored to their parents. Children were not supposed to be out after dark.

Samuel Chotzinoff, born in Russia in 1889, remembered his childhood on Stanton Street in Manhattan.

There was always excitement on Stanton Street from the time school let out until supper time, and for an hour or two between that meal and bedtime. Something was always happening, and our attention was continually being shifted from one excitement to another. "What's a matter?" was a perpetual query as we were attracted by a sudden frantic exodus from a tenement, the clang of an ambulance as it drew up in front of a house, a person desperately running, pursued by a crowd, a runaway horse and wagon, a policeman forcibly propelling a drunk and twisting his arm until the wretch screamed with pain, an altercation through open windows between next-door neighbors.… There were no bells or letterboxes in the entrance corridors of the tenements on Stanton Street. The mailman blew a whistle in the downstairs hall and called out names in a voice loud enough to be heard even on the fifth floor, and the people would come running downstairs to get their letters.…

Every day after supper I would beg to be allowed to play for a while in front of the house, where I could be seen from our windows and, at the proper time, summoned to bed. Between sundown and evening, on fair days, Stanton Street had an enchantment of its own. The dying sun benevolently lacquered the garish red-brick buildings, softly highlighting a window, a cornice, a doorway. We would play on the sidewalks and in the gutter until the air grew dark and we could barely tell who was who. Then the lamplighter would emerge from the Bowery, carrying his lighted stick in one hand and a small ladder in the other. In the light of the gas lamps we played leapfrog over the empty milk cans in front of the grocery store. Each of us would vault over a single can and then, if successful, augment the vault over as many as seven cans! Or we would play hide-and-go-seek in the dim vestibules of the tenement houses.

In many cities, Jewish charitable organizations opened community centers to provide activities for children. Here, children from the Bertha Fensterwald Center in Nashville, Tennessee, take part in a citywide spring festival in 1920. They represent the Ben Lindauer park, which was next to the Fensterwald Center.

A woman sells eggs on Hester Street around 1895. This way of making a living was preferable to working in a sweatshop because the seller retained all the profits of her work.

A children's stand on Maxwell Street in Chicago, around 1890, sells such items as caramel apples and hard candies.

Dora Levine, shown here with her daughter Esther in 1910, owned the Pacific Fish Company in Portland, Oregon.

South Portland, Oregon, became a neighborhood of eastern European Jews at the end of the 19th century. Frieda Gass Cohen recalled:

When we grew up in South Portland, that area housed practically every Orthodox Jewish person in the city. There were very few who lived anyplace else. It was really a teeming place for Jews and what an exciting place! They brought up their children there; they educated them; they sent them to Hebrew school.... The children grew up in the neighborhood and more or less stayed in the neighborhood.... You were at home in ten houses on the block. You could knock on any door or you would not even have to knock; you could just open the door and walk into so many homes. Everyone in the neighborhood looked out for you. You could send your child out to play and it couldn't get hurt or mistreated because someone else's mother was always looking out to see that nobody hurt it. Everybody knew who you were. We were close to our neighbors.

Yes, our house was literally very close to that of our neighbors. Our windows were right next door to those of Abraham Rosencrantz's. That was all right because he was the chazzan [cantor] of the Sixth Street Synagogue...and he had a most beautiful voice. In the summer we would open our windows and he would open his windows and we could hear him practice davening [praying]. It was a pleasure.

Sophie Ruskay described her childhood experiences on the Lower East Side of Manhattan at the turn of the 20th century.

Children owned the streets in a way unthinkable to city children of today. There were a few parks, but too distant to be of any use, and so the street was the common playground. The separation of the boys and girls so rigidly carried on in the public schools also held on the streets; *boys played with boys, girls with girls.* Occasionally we girls might stand on the sidelines and watch the boys play their games, but usually our presence was ignored. There was no doubt about it, girls were considered inferior creatures. The athletic girl, the girl who would fearlessly decide on a career or even demand the right to study a profession, was still unknown. Teaching alone was grudgingly admitted as being "respectable" for a girl. Going to college was the rare achievement for a few hardy souls, but for most, it was only a dream. We knew it to be a boy's world, but we didn't seem to mind too much. We shared the life of the street unhampered by our parents who were too busy to try to mold us into a more respectable pattern. If we lacked the close supervision of the genteel world of maids and governesses, we gloried all the more in our freedom from restriction.

We girls played only girls' games. Tagging after us sometimes were our little brothers and sisters whom we were supposed to mind, but that was no great hardship or hindrance. We would toss them our bean bags, little cloth containers filled with cherry pits. "Now see that you play here on the stoop or you won't get any ice cream when the hokeypokey man comes along." The hope of getting that penny's worth of ice cream dished out on a bit of brown paper was sufficient to quell any incipient revolt on the part of our little charges. Thus unhampered, we could proceed to our game of potsy. Mama didn't like me to play potsy. She thought it "disgraceful" to mark up our sidewalk with chalk for our lines and boxes; besides, hopping on one foot and pushing the thick piece of tin, I managed to wear out a pair of shoes in a few weeks! I obeyed her wishes in my own way, by playing farther down the street and marking up someone else's sidewalk.

Neither my friends nor I played much with dolls. Since families generally had at least one baby on hand, we girls had plenty of opportunity to shower upon the baby brothers or sisters the tenderness and love that would otherwise have been diverted to dolls. Besides, dolls were expensive.

Max Teicher came to the United States in August 1913 and settled on the Lower East Side of New York.

When I started to make a little money I was living as a boarder, but I got tired of it. You know, the woman has three rooms on Essex Street or some other little street downtown and she would keep two or three people. Besides sleeping, she would feed them and do their laundry. She would put up single beds and sofas and all that in three rooms, including the kitchen. This is the way I lived, and it was not easy. Not that we were used to much better; at least I was not, and I didn't mind it so much. But the bugs, the bedbugs would eat you alive. From one place to another you moved figuring here is going to be better; but it was not.... Maybe the price was even a little higher, so even if you made an extra two dollars a week you paid it out in rent.

Marie Jastrow came from Serbia in 1907. Her family settled in an ethnically mixed neighborhood in New York City. In her Memoirs, *she described the importance of the El, or elevated railroad.*

We moved again, to a flat [apartment] with its own bathroom, on Ninety-second Street near First Avenue, and stayed over the winter. We were beginning to get adjusted to our new life, which was no longer so bewildering as it had seemed on that first day in Ninth Street. My parents were even growing accustomed to marvels like the horsecar and the elevated train. I do not remember horsecars in Yarac [the village in Serbia where she grew up]. Certainly there were no elevated trains.

The El carried my father to and from his job every day. After a while the ride on the El became a kind of social gathering. There were greetings, handclasps and laughing faces when a familiar figure boarded the train. My father loved those social train rides every morning. If this seems strange today, one must remember that New York in that immigrant period was filled

Newly killed ducks and loaves of bread are for sale at this outdoor stand on the Lower East Side in 1895. Prices were often agreed on after haggling between buyer and seller.

A scene in 1927 at the East Lombard Street market in Baltimore, Maryland.

Bathgate Avenue in the Bronx, the northernmost borough of New York City, in 1936.

Many of the Jewish immigrants from eastern Europe lived in cramped tenement apartments. In the hot summer months, people used their fire escapes for sleeping or merely to get some fresh air.

with people who came from somewhere else. Alone, without family, their need was for new alliances and friendships. They needed companionship, even if only on the El.

Lifelong relationships often resulted from these rides. Sometimes friendships stemming from the El led to home invitations. There were always daughters in the house, and before you knew it there was a marriage.

Love indeed bloomed in the immigrant Jewish neighborhoods. Sadie Frowne told an interviewer in 1902 about a man she met in the clothing factory where she worked in Brooklyn.

Henry is tall and dark, and he has a small mustache. His eyes are brown and large. He is pale and much educated, having been to school. He knows a great many things and has some money saved. I think nearly $400. He is not going to be in a sweatshop all the time, but will soon be in the real estate business, for a lawyer that knows him well has promised to open an office and pay him to manage it.

Henry has seen me home every night for a long time.... He wants me to marry him, but I am not 17 yet, and I think that is too young. He is only 19, so we can wait.

I have been to the fortune teller's three or four times, and she always tells me that though I have had such a lot of trouble I am to be very rich and happy. I believe her because she has told me so many things that have come true. So I will keep on working in the factory for a time. Of course it is hard, but I would have to work hard even if I was married....

The machines are all run by foot-power, and at the end of the day one feels so weak that there is a great temptation to lie right down and sleep. But you must go out and get air, and have some pleasure. So instead of lying down I go out, generally with Henry. Sometimes we go to Coney Island, where there are good dancing places, and sometimes we go to Ulmer Park to picnics. I am very fond of dancing, and, in fact, all sorts of pleasure. I go to the theater quite often, and like those plays that make you cry a great deal. "The Two Orphans" is good. Last time I saw it I cried all night because of the hard times that the children had in the play. I am going to see it again when it comes here....

Some of the women blame me very much because I spend so much money on clothes. They say that instead of a dollar a week I ought not to spend more than 25 cents a week on clothes, and that I should save the rest. But a girl must have clothes if she is to go into good society at Ulmer Park or Coney Island or the theater. Those who blame me are the country people who have old-fashioned notions, but the people who have been here a long time know better. A girl who does not dress well is stuck in a corner, even if she is pretty, and Aunt Fanny says that I do just right to put on plenty of style.

Theodore White, a journalist and author, described the Jewish neighborhood in Boston where he grew up in the 1920s.

Storekeepers had transformed Erie Street from the quiet residential neighborhood my grandparents had sought... into a semipermanent bazaar. Whatever you wanted you could buy on Erie Street. Or else someone could get it for you....

But it was the peddlers who gave the street its sound and motion. The banana man was Italian, but all other peddlers were Jewish. Early in the morning, the peddlers would go to their stables, hitch up their horses, and proceed to Faneuil Hall or the Fish Pier to bring back the day's glut in the city market. Then, leading their horse-and-wagons through Erie Street, they would yodel and chant their wares. For each peddler another chant: the fish man would sing in a special voice: "Lebediker fisch, weiber, lebediker fisch" ["lovely fish, women, lovely fish"]; the Italian banana man would chorus only "Bananas, bananas, bananas," hawking a fruit previously unknown to Eastern Europeans.

Saturday night was the night of the fair. Friday was normally payday for the garment- and shoe-workers of the district, and Saturday was Shabbas. Thus Saturday night, when Sabbath was over, became shopping night—wives dragging their husbands after them, children skipping about the crowded corners, the women greeting each other, sharing gossip, the fathers stolidly enjoying themselves, the peddlers yelling their wares. Summer was best; the peddlers would bring in strange delights they had found in the Faneuil Hall produce market, and Jews could see for perhaps the first time wagons of watermelons (25 cents each), pineapple wagons, grape wagons, as well as wagons full of rejected or factory-surplus socks, shirts, undergarments.

When Arthur Goldberg was 77, the former Supreme Court justice and ambassador to the United Nations recalled the Chicago neighborhood where he grew up.

The neighborhood was called the Old West Side and it centered around Maxwell Street, where the bazaars were.... You see, you must remember Jews came from all over, and *bazaar* is a term used in the Middle East. It was a bunch of secondhand stores which were open on Sunday because Orthodox Jews could not open on Saturday....

There were stalls, secondhand shops, hookers [people employed by the shops to drag customers off the street] who tried to pull you in, all kinds of merchandise, from suits to vegetables and so on. And Jews who felt very inferior. They were afraid to go to the big stores, but they spoke Yiddish here; they could go here. And they felt more comfortable. And also it was very social. You argued with the proprietor. He knew a great many of the people and you haggled, but in a department store you had to pay one price. This was a familiar atmosphere. I never had a suit until I became Bar Mitzvah ["son of the commandment": a Jewish young man after his coming-of-age ceremony], and to get a Bar Mitzvah suit of course you went to Maxwell Street.

As Others Saw Them

A journalist described the tenements of the Lower East Side in a 1888 edition of the American Magazine:

They are great prison-like structures of brick, with narrow doors and windows, cramped passages and steep rickety stairs. They are built through from one street to the other with a somewhat narrower building connecting them.... The narrow court-yard...in the middle is a damp foul-smelling place, supposed to do duty as an airshaft; had the foul fiend designed these great barracks they could not have been more villainously arranged to avoid any chance of ventilation.... In case of fire they would be perfect death-traps, for it would be impossible for the occupants of the crowded rooms to escape by the narrow stairways, and the flimsy fire-escapes...are so laden with broken furniture, bales and boxes that they would be worse than useless. In the hot summer months...these fire-escape balconies are used as sleeping rooms by the poor wretches who are fortunate enough to have windows opening upon them.

Sam Millis's Market Stand in Philadelphia, around 1960.

A poster for one of the many Yiddish theaters in New York City. There were also Yiddish theaters in Chicago, Philadelphia, Newark, Boston, Baltimore, Cleveland, Detroit, St. Louis, and Los Angeles.

The cast of The Broken Hearts, *a play produced in 1903 at the Grand Theatre in New York City. Jacob Adler, the star, (seated at right in the first row) was one of the most popular Yiddish actors.*

THE YIDDISH THEATER

Samuel Chotzinoff, who grew up on the Lower East Side of New York City at the beginning of the 20th century, recalled the lively plays that featured Jacob and Sarah Adler, two of the best-known Yiddish actors.

Adler was highly effective in...those comedy dramas which portrayed the difficulties of emigrants from the Old World in becoming adjusted to the American scene. These plays, known to us as *lebensbilder* (portraits from life),...were perhaps the most popular type of drama on the East Side....

[One] play dealt with the familiar theme, with Mr. and Mrs. Adler attempting to hold the balance between Jewish orthodoxy, in the person of a pious old grandfather, and rebellion and Americanization, as represented by their teen-age son and daughter. In scene after scene, the young people scoffed at religion, at parental and grandparental authority.... The young daughter would always wind up her defiance of the Old World and her defense of the New with the memorable words: "This is the *United States of America, that's all.*" Her brother, sporting a wing collar, a fancy vest, and a straw hat with a string attached, interspersed American expressions in his speech.... "Dont'cha know" concluded every sentence. And "Go chase yourself."... Of course, we knew that the young people would get into trouble, the girl romantically, the youth through his association with godless, thoroughly Americanized "bums and loafers," as his grandfather called them. The climax arrived at the moment of their contrition.

Sara Abrams, the daughter of Polish immigrants, recalled the importance of the Yiddish theater of her youth.

Mother took us to see the various stock company shows, playing in Yiddish. Most of them dealt with life in the old country, particularly of life on the farm. Also of the love affairs of the children brought up in these lowlands. The father was usually depicted as the one they looked up to, as the law, and he ruled his family with a whip. It was called a *kanchik,* and just showing it was enough to command obedience....

When some women heard of a good play, with a moral to it, that would teach husbands how to act to their wives, or point out a fault in certain types of men, they would urge their friends to take their husbands along. They would nudge each other when the point was brought out in the play. Hoping that it took "effect" on their mates, they would glance on their expressionless faces to see whether it had "hit home."... But if one could not have a good cry at the show, it wasn't considered a very good show....

Everyone wore their holiday clothes, which they hoarded against just such an occasion. *Shiddachim* [matchmakings] were often the excuse for urging a young man or young woman to buy a ticket for the occasion, so that possible mates could see you "quite unexpectedly." And more likely than not, the entire family of either or both sides were present to "eye" the prospect; no item of wearing apparel was overlooked, and in the case of a young lady, she was sure to wear her best—furs by all means, if one had them, and diamond rings and scarf-pins were sported by the young men.

Ludwig Satz was a Yiddish comedian. In 1926, he wrote an article for the New York Times *about the Yiddish theater.*

The Yiddish audience...knows exactly what it goes to the theater to buy. It is intense about the play and its performance as the playwright and the actor. It is a hearty, zestful, passionate collaborator. It is a homogenous audience and it knows the life that its theater portrays. You cannot fool its members with false types and with false interpretations.... Hence, if you make the mistake of giving them something they don't identify...God forgive you.

But if you are what they want and if you did fit their prejudices and their understanding, no people in the world reward you with such enthusiasm. You may become anything from a hero to a savior.... And you feel that you have earned your reward, because you realize they know and are the character you are playing. He is in the audience by the hundred. You are a glass for many faces.

As Others Saw Them

The New York World *described a Yiddish theater called the Romania Opera House in 1891:*

Prison courtyards, nihilistic secret meeting places, dungeons, palaces, and other interesting places are made the scenes of such hair-raising happenings as terrible hand-to-hand battles, single combats and mysterious trials. Soldiers, rapists, nihilists, detectives, lovely conspirators in red silk skirts, who sing patriotic songs and revile the czar (amid tremendous applause from the audience).... At last in a great prison scene all come to violent deaths after a terrific ten minutes of active work with pistols, swords, and deadly poison. This absolutely horrifying climax is promptly followed by a parade of New York's foreign citizens, all in red, white and blue regalia and red flannel yachting caps, who are headed by a brass band playing "The Star Spangled Banner" to the cheering audience.

A scene from The Jewish Heart, *by Joseph Latimer, produced at Kessler's Thalia Theatre in New York in 1908.*

Abraham Jacobs and his wife. Jacobs was the hazan, or cantor, of the Congregation of the Sons of Israel in Providence, Rhode Island, from 1862 to 1869.

FAMILY

Emily Fechheimer Seasongood was born in Cincinnati in 1867 to a moderately wealthy German Jewish family. At 63 she recalled the activities of her childhood.

I enjoyed watching my dear mother in her various duties around the house. She had great artistic talent, designed and sewed dresses, and I often wanted to assist her, and she would give me bits of goods (calico in those days) and a needle. My dear mother was a very refined, intelligent, accomplished woman, and her circle of acquaintances was of like manner.... The ladies met at each other's homes, sewed and discussed literature, and the like, but not much gossiping took place. Children were never allowed in the room except to say "good day," and when there was an entertainment, it was furnished by the school children and was considered a great event. Many children came before the footlights, bowed, and had to repeat a sentence many times over before being able to finish reciting the poem or whatever part might have been assigned to them, but the parents, nevertheless, enjoyed it and thought them wonderful....

My dear sister was compelled to take me with her wherever she went, even though there were fourteen months' difference in our ages, and she was always much older in her ways than I, and her companions also. But my dear mother would say:

Nathan Falk, his wife, Rose, and their five children in Boise, Idaho, around 1890. Falk arrived from Germany in 1864. He and two brothers started a dry goods store and grocery, and branches of Falk's Idaho Department Store are still operating today.

"*Nimm es mit*" (Yiddish for "Take her with you"), meaning me, and so I trotted along, much to her regret. My sister and I were always dressed alike. I presume it was easier to buy enough of one piece of goods to make two dresses and cut them out of the same piece, than be choosing another kind. Besides, the stock was not as large in the shops then as in the present day. Every week my sister and I received one penny together, for which we were allowed to buy candy, which was of the purest and simplest production....

My sister and I were supplied with all sorts of games, and I did enjoy the Fridays nights and holidays when we were allowed to play them.... We had a large bowl of choice apples, nuts, and salted peas on a table, which we could partake of after finishing our games. One of the most interesting toys we possessed was a picture-show which was on a stand and looked somewhat like a circus tent, and had to be twirled to show the pictures in the inside of it; the pictures were changed every little while.

Rabbi Abraham Goodman with his wife, Ida, and their family in 1912. He was the first rabbi of Congregation B'nai Abraham in Butler, Pennsylvania.

Seeing that their children found suitable spouses was an important concern of Jewish parents. Harriet Lane Levy, who grew up in a middle-class home in turn-of-the-century San Francisco, remembered that time.

I knew that there were old maids; a cousin was fast becoming one. I heard my mother reproach her on her 21st birthday, but that did not mean that a girl would not eventually marry; it meant only that she would have to go to the country to live, to the interior....

Shopkeepers came to the city from the interior, from towns of the San Joaquin or Sacramento valleys, or from the mining towns...to buy goods. Their quest often included a sentimental hope, confided to a downtown wholesale merchant. If a man's appearance was agreeable and his credit good, he would be invited to the merchant's home to dine and meet the unmarried daughters. To my way of thinking the interior was broad enough to take care of every unmated daughter....

Everybody agreed that August Friedlander was a fitting alliance for Addie [Harriet's sister]. Although still a young man (he was 26), he had a good business in a growing town across the bay. Father made inquiries of the merchants from whom August bought his goods, and they all agreed upon his integrity and good credit.... Levi Strauss, the millionaire manufacturer of I X L Overalls [as Levi's jeans were called then], told Father that he was the brains of the business.

Both Father and Mother agreed that he was better qualified than any other suitor who had yet appeared, and they encouraged him to come often. At later visits the family retired, the brother was omitted, and August and Addie conversed behind the closed folding doors.

"Well?" Father asked after a month. "What do you say?"

"I like him," Addie said, and within 24 hours I was hurrying to the neighbors, announcing the betrothal and spreading

Dr. Moses Behrend, his wife, Clara, and their daughter Ruth in an early automobile around 1905 in Philadelphia.

The Straus Family

In 1854, two years after Lazarus Straus arrived in the United States, he sent his wife in Germany enough money to bring their three young sons across the ocean. That marked the foundation of a distinguished American family.

Twenty years later, Lazarus Straus's two elder sons, Isidor and Nathan, became partners in the R. H. Macy store in New York, eventually becoming sole owners. The retail business formed the basis of a family fortune. Isidor also served as a member of Congress and as president of the Educational Alliance, which opened schools, libraries, and summer camps for immigrant children. During the depression of 1892–94, Nathan distributed coal and food to New York's poor and opened boardinghouses that charged five cents for a bed and a meal. He also contributed to Jewish health-care facilities in what was then Palestine. A town in Israel is named after him.

Lazarus Straus's youngest son, Oscar, earned a law degree from Columbia University and became active in political affairs. He became the first Jewish American cabinet officer when President Theodore Roosevelt appointed him secretary of commerce and labor in 1906. Oscar Straus was also one of the founders of the American Jewish Committee, which was formed to oppose persecution of Jews in Russia.

In 1893, Isidor Straus's son Jesse Isidor graduated from Harvard University. He became president of Macy's in 1919 and turned it into the world's largest department store. President Franklin D. Roosevelt appointed him ambassador to France in 1933, and his son Jack Isidor took over the leadership of Macy's.

Nathan Straus's son Nathan, Jr., went into journalism, and in the late 1930s became president of the New York radio station WMCA. His son Peter purchased additional radio and television stations to form the Straus Broadcasting Group.

Oscar Straus's son Roger W. Straus married the daughter of another prominent Jewish American family, the Guggenheims, and became president of the Guggenheim-owned mineral refining business. Roger W. Straus was a founder of the National Conference of Christians and Jews in 1928. His son, Roger W. Straus, Jr., cofounded the book publishing company that is now Farrar Straus & Giroux.

consternation in the homes of marriageable daughters down the two blocks.

Harry Golden, who would become the editor of The Carolina Israelite *newspaper, came to New York in 1905 as a two-year-old. He remembered the importance of family in his youth on the Lower East Side.*

In the Jewish household the father was a figure of authority, the boss. This meant that no one sat down to the dinner table until he came home from work and that we did not speak until he spoke first or until he had asked us a question. Jews call this *derekh eretz,* a phrase literally translated as the "custom of the land." In actual usage it means respect for elders and particularly for parents. Mother made all the decisions but she was always obedient to the idea of *derekh eretz.* Alone, she would tell my father, "I found a new apartment on Ludlow Street. I paid a deposit and I've asked the moving van to come Monday." That evening at the dinner table during a lull she would say, "Children, pay attention. Papa has something very important to say to you." Father would proceed to describe the move next Monday and Mother would listen through the whole process as though hearing it for the first time, even congratulating him afterward on his excellent judgment.

Rose Cohen, an immigrant daughter, remembered how her mother started to adjust her style to American ways.

Mother had been here only a short time when I noticed that she looked older and more old-fashioned than father. I noticed that it was so with most of our women, especially those that wore wigs or kerchiefs on their heads. So I thought that if I could persuade her to leave off her kerchief she would look younger and more up-to-date. [The Mishnah instructed married women not to appear outside the home with their hair visible in order not to distract men from study or prayer.]...

So, one day, when I happened to be at home and the children were playing in the yard, and we two were alone in the house, I asked her playfully to take off her kerchief and let me do her hair, just to see how it would look. She consented reluctantly. She had never before in her married life had her head uncovered before anyone. I took off her kerchief and began to fuss with her hair....

I was surprised how different she looked. I had never before known what a fine broad forehead my mother had, nor how soft were her blue-gray eyes, set rather deep and far apart. I handed her our little mirror from Cherry Street. She glanced at herself, admitted frankly that it looked well, and began hastily to put on her kerchief as if she feared being frivolous too long. I caught hold of her hands.

"Mama," I coaxed, "please don't put the kerchief on again—ever!"

When father came home in the evening and caught sight of her while still at the door, he stopped and looked at her with astonishment. "What!" he cried, half earnestly, half jestingly. "Already you are becoming an American lady!" Mother looked abashed for a moment; in the next, to my surprise and delight, I heard her brazen it out in her quiet way.

"As you can see," she said, "I am not staying far behind."

Charles Angoff went from Russia to Boston at the beginning of the 20th century. He described his father's attempt to maintain the ways of the old country.

My father looked upon ice cream as on the whole a shameful thing, and as children's food at best. Whenever he'd see any of his children eat it—and we did manage to get a cone of strawberry or vanilla or chocolate ice cream every now and then, largely through the connivance of our mother—he'd look at one condescendingly and say, "A strange place, America, a very strange place!" As for low shoes, they simply made no sense to him. He couldn't understand anybody wearing them. "Don't they fall off?" he once asked a neighbor who had been here for about ten years. All of us boys wore high shoes till we began to earn our own money. My father never gave in. As for ketchup, he was sure it wasn't kosher, no matter how many rabbis' signatures were on the bottle, and he considered it as fit only for pigs, anyway. "I wouldn't wish it upon the worst Russian hooligan," he said.

The movies he didn't care for at all. During his first five years in this county, he went only once to a silent movie, and then only to please my mother and us kids. When we left the movie house—the picture was *Orphans of the Storm* with the Gish sisters—he spat on the sidewalk, turned to my mother and, with stern face, said, "There's no telling where next you'll want me to go. I won't do it, I'm telling you that now!"

My mother merely said, "Not so loud. Be quiet." After that, she took us to the movies by herself. But for years he argued with her about it. He sensed something immoral in the whole art of motion pictures and even something atheistical, though he never made these charges openly. That would have reflected upon his family.

In respect to celery and lettuce.... For years he wouldn't allow them in the house. "This is a house for human beings," he said, "not for cows and animals that eat anything that grows. Pooh!"

In impoverished households, family tragedies were common. One was the desertion of the father. Each week the Jewish Daily Forward *published "The Gallery of Missing Men," with notes provided by wives and relatives.*

Max: The children and I now say farewell to you. You left us in such a terrible state. You had no compassion for us.... Have you ever asked yourself why you left us? Max, where is your conscience?... I was a young, edu-

In strictly Orthodox Jewish families, the mother often takes the dominant role in raising the children. Ideally the father is engaged in study. Eva Broido, an immigrant from Lithuania at the end of the 19th century, remembered:

Our father, a kind and not unintelligent man, looked upon us children as something extraneous, with which he would not concern himself. He was an unworldly Talmudic scholar, who needed little for himself and knew nothing of our needs.... It was left to our mother to provide for us all.

Joseph and Anna Gartner and their children in 1923. The Gartners were the first Jewish residents of Castle Shannon, Pennsylvania.

Abraham Cohen (behind the second row, with hat and suit) with many family members at a picnic in Milwaukee in 1919.

Rebecca Brodek Harris, who arrived in San Francisco in the early 1850s, with her daughter, granddaughter, and great-granddaughter.

cated, decent girl when you took me. You lived with me for six years during which time I bore you four children, and then you left me. Of the four children, only two remain, but you have made them living orphans. Who will bring them up? Who will support us? Have you no pity for your own flesh and blood? Consider what you are doing. My tears choke me and I cannot write any more.

The conflict between the ways of the old country and the new American ways was fought out within the family. Often family members sought answers through letters to the advice column of the Forward—*the Bintel Brief, Yiddish for "a bundle of letters."*

I am a girl 16 years old. I live together with my parents and two older sisters. Last year I met a young man. We love one another. He is a very respectable man, and makes a fine living. My sisters have no fiances. I know that should I marry they will never talk to me. My parents are also strongly against it since I am the youngest child. I do not want to lose my parents' love, and neither do I want to lose my lover because this would break my heart. Give me some advice, dear Editor! What shall I do? Shall I leave my parents and marry my sweetheart, or shall I stay with my parents and lose the happiness of my life? Give me some advice, dear Editor!

Journalist Theodore White remembered a division in his family when he was a boy in the 1920s. His grandparents lived upstairs in the family's house.

Upstairs was Yiddish-speaking. Downstairs, we spoke English. Upstairs, Friday night, the eve of Shabbas, was celebrated with candles, wine and challah, the twisted white bread. Downstairs, my father sat adamant—he, the unbeliever, had come to see religion as a superstition and would have no part of its ceremonies. I was a pawn between the two families, moved by my grandmother's tyrannical will and my mother's desire to please her mother and her husband at the same time. I rather enjoyed it all.

Then I would be called upstairs for the prayers of the Kiddush [Sabbath ceremony]. I would make the traditional blessing in Hebrew, and would be given a goblet of red wine.

The novelist Philip Roth described the generational conflicts in his boyhood neighborhood of Newark, New Jersey.

Our parents were, with few exceptions, the first-generation offspring of poor turn-of-the-century immigrants from Galicia and Polish Russia, raised in predominantly Yiddish-speaking Newark households.... However unaccented and American-sounding their speech, however secularized their own beliefs...they were influenced still by their childhood training and by strong parental ties to what often seemed to us antiquated, socially useless old-country mores and perceptions.

My larger boyhood society cohered around the most inherently American phenomenon at hand—the game of baseball, whose mystique was encapsulated in three relatively inexpensive fetishes that you could have always at your side in your room, not only while you did your homework but in bed with you while you slept if you were a worshiper as primitive as I was at ten and eleven: They were a ball, a bat, and a glove. The solace that my Orthodox grandfather doubtless took in the familiar leathery odor of the flesh-worn straps of the old phylacteries [little boxes that Orthodox Jewish men wear on their left arm and forehead while praying] in which he wrapped himself each morning, I derived from the smell of my mitt, which I ritualistically donned every day to work a little on my pocket. I was an average playground player, and the mitt's enchantment had to do less with foolish dreams of becoming a major leaguer, or even a high school star, than with the bestowal of membership in a great nationalistic church from which nobody had ever seemed to suggest that Jews should be excluded.

Carol Ascher grew up in Kansas, the daughter of parents who had fled Nazi Germany. She described her family's insistence on keeping certain traditional ways.

I could make a list of things we did and didn't do "*bei uns,*" [Yiddish for "among our kind"].... *Bei uns* there were no comic books, chewing gum, soda pop, or spongy white bread; we did not come to the table in pajamas or with uncombed hair; frilly dresses that wore out in one season and patent leather shoes were beneath us (though longed for by all three of us sisters); leaving the family radio on a rock 'n roll station took a unified political siege by us when we reached our teens. *Bei uns* one got good grades in school, even though my father could not be impressed by seeing them and inevitably upped the ante by insisting that he preferred a good moral character to merely smarts. Perhaps *bei uns* one always upped the ante, even on oneself.

The wedding of Labe H. Golden and Bessie Antweil in Fort Worth, Texas, in 1924.

Abraham Lapping and his wife at their home in Colchester, Connecticut, in 1940. They were dairy farmers in a rural area but kept in touch with the Jewish American community by subscribing to a Yiddish newspaper.

I attended Hebrew school on 116th Street in Harlem from age six to age twelve. There was no formal graduation, and in those days there were no bas mitzvahs [the equivalent, for girls, of a boy's bar mitzvah]. Hebrew school was very important. I had to learn to read Hebrew, to pray, to know a little Hebrew, so that when I grew up I would be able to pass this heritage on to the next generation.

Although this man lived in a coal cellar in a New York City tenement, he prepared for the Sabbath dinner by buying a braided loaf of bread. Called challah, this bread symbolizes the manna that God dropped for the Israelites to eat while they wandered in the desert.

RELIGIOUS RITUAL AND PRACTICES

Before the U.S. Civil War, the Kussy family came to the United States from Germany. They settled in Newark, New Jersey, then a rural area where they lived with non-Jewish Germans and Irish immigrants. One of the daughters, Sarah Kussy, remembered the importance of religion in her home.

In our home a religious spirit prevailed. Upon entering the house one could tell immediately that he was in a Jewish home. Prominent on one of the walls was a large *mizrekh* (a drawing or picture on the east wall) [to mark the direction of prayer to Israel], with the legend in Hebrew, "From the rising of the sun unto its setting, the Lord's name is to be praised," and profusely illustrated with Biblical motives. We were taught little Hebrew prayers before we were able to articulate clearly. We also learned German prayers that mother had repeated as a child and were taught the *brokhes* (blessings) for various occasions....

The *seder* (festive commemorative meal) on Passover was an eagerly anticipated event. Preparations for it began weeks ahead. Even the children were drawn into these activities. We cleaned out boxes and bureau drawers, turned pockets inside out, followed father about as he *batteled khomets* (searched for leavened food on the evening before Passover), helped to change the dishes, prepared the *kharoses* (a condiment of nuts, apples and other spices used at the *seder*), and arranged the *seder* dish....

On *Rosh Hashonah* [New Year's Day in the Jewish calendar] it was our custom to write New Year's letters to our parents and place them under their plates on the eve of the festival. This custom has survived among some members of the family to this day....

Father had a strong sense of identification with the hopes and aspiration of *klal ysroel*, universal Israel. He was more than just an American Jew; all Israel was his concern, its future as well as its past. I recall a day when father came into the room with an open copy of the *Staatszeitung* [a Jewish newspaper] in his hand: "I have just read," he said in German, "that a school has been opened in Jaffa, Palestine, with Hebrew as the medium of instruction." Then, with eyes aglow and voice thrilled with emotion, he burst forth, "I would go through fire and water for Israel. Some day it will come," he added prophetically, "that we shall possess Palestine. It may come in a perfectly natural way. We may have to buy the land." Revival of the Hebrew language, Jewish national life, Palestine—the connection was clear to father. And this was before [Theodor]

Herzl [father of modern Zionism] issued his call to the Jewish people and no one had heard of a Jewish National Fund.

Although my parents worked hard and had certain aspirations for their children, they were not interested in the pursuit of wealth.... Mother expressed her hopes for us in this way: "My children need not become wealthy. Let them remain good Jews."

Charles Angoff and his parents moved from Russia to Boston shortly after the turn of the 20th century. He described his Bar Mitzvah, or coming-of-age ceremony, held when a boy is 13. It is the first occasion when he is "called to the Torah," permitted to read it as part of the public ceremonies. The boy himself is also called Bar Mitzvah.

I was *Bar Mitzva* on Thursday. My father woke me up at 6:30 in the morning and took me to *shul* [synagogue]. There were about thirty people at the service. I was called to the Torah for the first time—and that was *Bar Mitzva*. Some of the congregants came over to me and wished me *mazel tov* [in Hebrew, "good luck," but more commonly used as an expression of congratulations]. My father bashfully put his arm

The Rudick family of Pittsburgh at a seder dinner in 1908. Baruch Rudick (center, wearing top hat), his wife, Elka, their children and spouses, and one grandchild are present.

Congregation Shaarie Torah of Portland, Oregon, built the first Orthodox synagogue in the Northwest in 1902. Shown here are members of the choir around 1919.

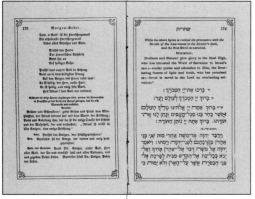

Prayers are printed in English, German, and Hebrew in this prayer book, entitled The Divine Service of American Israelites for the Day of Atonement, *by Isaac M. Wise. The book was published in Cincinnati in 1866.*

around me and also congratulated me. Then he and I walked a bit and he went off to work. I turned toward home feeling terribly lonely. I had become a full, mature Jew—and most of Boston was asleep, and didn't care. The few people who passed me on the street didn't care either. When I reached our house, as soon as I put my hand on the doorknob my mother opened the door and threw her arms around me and kissed me and hugged me and kissed me again. Her arm around me, she took me to the kitchen, and there on the table was the *Shabbes* tablecloth. To my mother it was *yom tov* [a holiday celebration]. She had the usual *boolkes* [small challah rolls] on a platter, but there was also a platter of the kind of cinnamon cakes I liked, and a smaller platter of ginger jam, another favorite of mine. Also a cup of cocoa. "Eat, Shayel, eat," said my mother. I suggested she have some cocoa too. "No, I'm not hungry." I ate. I was conscious that she was looking at me with great appreciation of what had happened to me. Her oldest son was now a full man in Israel. I was embarrassed, but I was also delighted. I finished my cocoa, and mother said, "Have another cup." The last time she had suggested I have another cup of cocoa was when I was convalescing from a cold that had almost turned into pneumonia. I had another cup. When I was finished with my special breakfast, mother said, "Father had to go to work. He had to. You understand."

"Sure," I said.

"But we'll have a small reception on Saturday night, after *mincha* [afternoon prayer service]. We've invited the relatives and some friends. So we'll have a little reception."

"Oh," I said, too moved to say anything else.

She got up, came to me, patted my head and then kissed me slowly. "Maybe you're a little sleepy, Shayel. Maybe you want to sleep a little more. I'll wake you up in time for school."

"Yes, I think I'll have a little more sleep," I said.

I didn't want any more sleep. I lay down on the bed. I was profoundly happy. Everything was good. Everything was very good.

Samuel Rosinger came to the United States from Hungary and was ordained a rabbi in 1910. After serving a congregation in Toledo, Ohio, for two years, he heard that Temple Emanuel of Beaumont, Texas, needed a rabbi. He applied for the position and was invited for a trial sermon.

It was a trial of the severest kind. To give that sermon, I had to travel over 1,200 miles in August, the hottest month in the South. My train missed connections in New Orleans, and I had to spend the night in the St. Charles Hotel—alas, not in peaceful slumber, but chasing mosquitoes. My room had no screens, but it had a four-poster bed, covered with a veil-like material. I thought that this was a colonial-style ornament, and being extremely tired, I removed the canopy covering, hit the pillow, and fell asleep. About midnight I awoke to the tune of a dissonant symphony emanating from a swarm of "skeeters"

A 1898 Purim party in Portland, Oregon. Purim, or the Feast of Lots, is one of the happiest holidays in the Jewish calendar. Children often dress up in costumes.

stinging my body and sucking my blood....

According to the train schedule, I was supposed to arrive at my destination Friday morning. Now, here was Friday morning, and I had before me a dusty all-day ride in a day coach on a train that stopped at every flag station. It finally lumbered into the station at Beaumont an hour and a half late. I was met at the depot by the president and treasurer of the congregation. They took me to a nearby hotel to brush up and whisked me to the temple. The sleepless night, the humid heat, and the long travel exhausted what I thought was my last ounce of energy, and if my exterior showed my limpness and languor, I must have cut a sorry figure when I ascended the pulpit. Before starting divine service, I am in the habit of turning to the ark and offering the supplication, "Heavenly Father, open the gates of heaven to our prayer." On this occasion I added the fervent prayer, "and give Thy faint servant strength to endure this trial." And the Good Lord answered my prayer. As soon as I started to read the service, I became oblivious to my fatigue and delivered my sermon with assurance and conviction in my voice. Sabbath morning I spoke to the women in a lighter vein, and Sunday I was elected for a term of two years.

When Faye Moskowitz was growing up in the 1920s, her parents did not strictly observe the Jewish dietary laws. But when she spent a summer with her cousin Esther, whose father was an Orthodox rabbi, she observed the care that families took to ensure that the food was strictly kosher.

They came to Esther's house sometimes, the women, late Thursday afternoons or early Friday mornings, carrying their Shabbes chickens wrapped in liver-colored

In many Reform Jewish congregations, a confirmation ceremony is held for graduates of the religious school. This is the confirmation class of 1956 at Temple Emanu-El in Miami Beach, Florida.

Strictly speaking, bar mitzvah *("son of the commandments") refers to any 13-year-old Jewish male. Many Jewish families celebrate the coming of age of a son with a bar mitzvah party like this one. Bat Mitzvah is the equivalent occasion for girls in Reform and Conservative congregations.*

butcher paper and leaking newsprint. Then my uncle, whom even his brothers spoke of as the Rabbi, wearing as always his stern black suit, would leave his study and solemnly escort [each Jewish woman] into my aunt Celia's kitchen....

The Rabbi washed his hands while the visitor unwrapped the chicken for him to examine. "See, Rabbi, when I went to kosher the chicken, I saw this blemish on its heart," or "What do you think, Rabbi? Look how the liver is so large and yellow." And my uncle, his tiny hooked nose slightly averted, would touch the organs with the tip of a carefully trimmed fingernail. Esther and I stood half hidden behind the pantry doorway, where I could catch underneath the scent of fresh dill and parsley from her mother's already simmering chicken soup, the visitor's rank sweat, the slightly sour stink of her yellow, waxy chicken....

I never had the courage to ask Esther if she sometimes wondered, as I did, whether her father took into account the shabbiness of a peeling handbag or a pair of shoes gone tipsy at the heels when he made his judgment....

Like as not, the Rabbi would find the chicken kosher and, tension broken, he, Esther's mother, and the woman would laugh and talk for a few minutes.

Solomon Blatt practiced law in Barnwell, South Carolina, from 1917 until the 1980s. He grew up in the small town of Blackville. At age 90, he recalled the difficulties of keeping up with religious duties and practices in an area of the country where there were few other Jewish families.

My parents were religious to the extent that my father went to Charleston and they taught him how to kill chickens [in a kosher manner] and all that. On the holidays, he closed [his store] and went to synagogue, either in Charleston or Augusta. I can remember, of course, Saturday they had to keep open because that's the only day they did any business. Some days he wouldn't take in ten dollars. He wouldn't smoke on Saturday. I remember this: my mother would come to the store to help and she would not tear the [wrapping] paper off the paper rack on Saturday. She'd make the customer do it.

It was difficult to maintain our Jewishness. When I was a child, Blackville had about 1500 to 2000 people. I'd say there were three or four Jewish families.

My mother and father tried their best to be kosher in everything that they did. They observed the holidays, sacred Jewish holidays. But it got to the point where they had to buy meat that wasn't kosher. My mother did the best she could under the circumstances. And I'll tell you one thing about it, there is one thing I am right proud of, and I'm that way, too: they didn't hesitate to let everybody know they were of the Jewish faith, and I think the public knew it generally, too.

Jacob Javits, who served as a U.S. senator from New York from 1957 to 1980, was born on the Lower East Side in 1904, the son of immigrants from eastern Europe. He remembered the importance of religious holidays.

On Friday evening, at the Sabbath meal, the father says kiddush, the blessing of the wine and bread. Earlier, when the mother lights the candles, she says her own blessing.

My mother welcomed and appreciated the Sabbath and the Holy Days as a respite from her daily grind. They provided a chance to spend a few extra hours with her family. To my father, however, religion meant much more. The rituals of orthodox Judaism were the core of his life; despite all of his life's vicissitudes, he never forgot his rabbinical training and never lost his passionate faith in the law of the Torah. Upon arising in the morning, he strapped to his forehead and to his left arm the little leather-bound *tefilin,* phylacteries, containing prayers and passages from the Torah. [Orthodox Jewish men wear these boxes on their left arm and forehead while praying.] Then, with these symbols of the Hebrew faith near his mind and his heart, he would pray. Except on the Sabbath and on Jewish holidays—which required of him longer, more intricate rituals and prayers—my father prayed with his phylacteries every morning of his life.

The wedding of H. Lew Zuckerman and Sadie Belle Goldberg in Beth Israel synagogue, Los Angeles, in 1909. The couple stands under a chuppa, *or canopy, which symbolizes the husband's house in which they will live.*

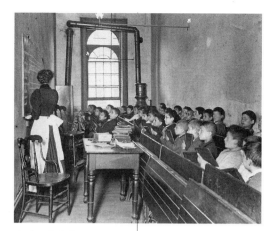

A crowded classroom in the Essex Market School on the Lower East Side of New York around 1890.

SCHOOL

Marie Jastrow came to New York from Serbia. She described how the immigrants eagerly embraced opportunities for education.

Never was there such an awakening in people of the desire for learning. The concern of parents for the education of the children was the most important element in their lives. It became a part of a belief in existing for the future, and never mind the present. Parents thought of only one thing, that their children would go to school, learn, and have a better life than they had....

As the children of newcomers, we understood well the uncertainties of the immigrant status. As a result, before anything else, we set to work to learn the new language. Actually, we had no choice. Teachers in my time had no qualms about deflating egos and were unconcerned about enhancing our "inner resources." They taught us relentlessly and thoroughly. Each teacher had forty of us in a class to contend with.... There was no time for special attention to slow learners. It was learn with the rest or stay behind.

Came an unsatisfactory report: "For this I crossed the ocean in steerage, so my son should be a nothing, a nobody?" "Take your books and study." "What, no homework? Study anyway! So you'll know what the teacher asks you tomorrow."...

Our parents had great admiration for teachers. This atti-

The Educational Alliance was founded in 1889 to assist new Jewish immigrants. The "Edgie" opened schools and summer camps for Lower East Side children. Here, the library at its headquarters is crowded with eager readers in 1898.

tude was so general that anything accomplished in the class-room was considered the highest of all achievements. And the teacher, who ruled in that dedicated place of learning, had the highest rank in parental esteem.

In his autobiography, Samuel Chotzinoff, born in Russia in 1889, recalled school on the Lower East Side in New York.

The children of Jewish immigrants kept their faith alive by studying Scripture and learning Hebrew. This is a scene from the Talmud school on Hester Street in 1889, when Jews from eastern Europe were starting to arrive.

It was out of the question for me to begin school without a pencil box and some other less important "supplies" that beckoned through the window of the candy store on our block.... Though I pleaded hard for a two-storied pencil box costing a quarter, my mother bought me a plain, oblong casket with a sliding top for ten cents. When our shopping was done, my supplies consisted of the pencil box, four writing pads at a penny each, and a set of colored blotters costing a nickel, the last wrung from my reluctant parent after I conjured up a class-room crisis in which the teacher would call for a show of blotters and I would be the only pupil unable to produce any. My mother had a horror of nonconformity, a failing I early spotted and often exploited.

On the first Monday in September my mother took me and my scanty supplies to school, where I was enrolled and given a desk and a seat in a large classroom. The teacher, a gray-haired, middle-aged lady, told us to call her Miss Murphy.... The name sounded alien and therefore forbidding, and might have been chosen to emphasize the natural barrier between teacher and pupil. She was obviously a pagan—a *Chreestch*—our name for any non-Jew. Miss Murphy read out our last names from a long paper in front of her, and we raised our hands to signify our presence.... By the following morning Miss Murphy, having already memorized the surnames of her entire class, called the roll without once referring to her paper.

She then went to the blackboard and in beautiful script wrote "Catt" and, looking over the sea of heads in front of her, said: "Something is wrong with the spelling of this word. Katzenelenbogen, stand up and tell me what is wrong." A small, skinny boy rose in the back of the room and said something in an indistinct voice. "Speak up, Katzenelenbogen!" Miss Murphy sharply commanded. My heart went out to Katzenelenbogen in his ordeal....

On promotion day the class arrived all scrubbed and neat, with hair combed and definitely parted, the labor of mothers who cherished a wild hope that in case of doubt an extra bit of cleanliness might tip the scales.... Tense, nervous, and dispirited, we went through our usual morning routine. At ten o'clock the monitors left their seats and opened the windows halfway with long poles while the class rose and exercised their arms and heads with Miss Murphy leading and commanding, "Inspire!—Expire!" the class noisily breathing in and out in response. At a quarter to twelve the room suddenly became unaccountably still. Miss Murphy seated herself by her desk, opened it, and drew out the promotion list. I could see the red

An orchestra at Congregation Bais Israel Anshoi Estrech in Providence, Rhode Island, around 1930.

Settlement houses were established in many cities to provide recreation and educational opportunities for immigrant children. This is a playground on the roof of the Irene Kaufmann Settlement in New York City in 1924.

line down the middle of the page, looking like a thin blood barrier, which separated the names on either side. Miss Murphy, before addressing herself to the list, was exasperatingly deliberate in tidying the top of her desk, arranging her pencils in a row, and moving the water glass with its little bouquet of flowers to one side. At last she was ready.

"I shall now read the promotion list," she announced. "As your names are called, rise and stand in the aisle. Those whose names are not called will remain seated.".... The class held its breath as Miss Murphy again gave her attention to the list. "Abramowitz," Miss Murphy intoned, and Abramowitz got to his feet precipitately and stood in the aisle....

We promoted boys, at a command from Miss Murphy, closed ranks and were marched into an adjacent classroom, where we found four dejected boys, the leftovers of our new grade. Miss Murphy made a formal farewell address and turned us over to Miss Applebaum, our new teacher. Then the bell rang and we marched into the street and scattered quickly to our homes, for once not loitering to talk and plan, in our eagerness to carry the good news to our families.

Attendance at schools and universities could cause problems, particularly for Orthodox Jews. Louis Geffen, who moved to Atlanta in 1911, remembered the difficulties.

It was necessary to make certain contacts in order to be able to attend Emory University, because at that time Emory University had classes on Saturday, and being Orthodox, we do not write on Saturday. And also, where we were living at the time, Emory University was about six miles distance and we don't ride on the sabbath, so it was a problem. At that time Bishop [Warren] Candler was the chancellor of Emory University, so Rabbi Geffen [Louis Geffen's father] had a conference with Bishop Candler and he told him what his problem was. Bishop Candler said, "Rabbi, we'd like to have your son attend Emory University. And I can tell you this, that he will not have to violate any of his religious precepts. But he will have to attend because the laws of Georgia require a certain number of days or hours of attendance that we have to certify that a student has attended before we can grant him a degree."

So my father said, "Will he have to do any writing?" He said, "No." [His father] said, "Will he be required to take examinations or tests on the sabbath or on religious holidays?" He said, "No, they will be given an opportunity to take it at some other time." And so they worked out something, and we had to walk the six miles on Saturday and on other religious holidays, which we did. We didn't have to do it but we wanted to do it, and we did it.

Leah Lifschitz was born in Brooklyn, the daughter of Jewish immigrants from the Ukraine. She was disappointed that she could not go to college.

I graduated from high school when I was 16. I had been skipping [grades] all along.

It was 1938 and the height of the great Depression. My mother and father were both working and we were struggling. Times were very, very hard. My sister was married and my brother, now a university professor, got through school on total scholarships. The fact that my brother went to college was a very big thing in our family. But he was really doing this on his own.

When it came to me, my father's values and my mother's values were different. My mother wanted me to continue my education. My father believed that girls just had to go out and work after a certain amount of time; they didn't need that much education.

This caused a tremendous conflict in my life. My peers also came from immigrant families, but one where values regarding education for girls were different. So my friends went on to college. This was something my father would not accept.

From the time I was sixteen until I was eighteen was the saddest period of my life. Because I graduated from high school at sixteen with an academic diploma, thinking of going to college.

When I went to grammar school for the first time, I spoke no English. I spoke only Yiddish because that was the language that my grandmother spoke and that was the language that I was brought up in. When I went to school, I was shocked to find that there were children who didn't speak Yiddish. It was the only language I knew.

—Harvey Teicher, born to immigrant parents in Brooklyn in 1919

Young Jewish immigrants learned trades that would help them find jobs. This is a cooking class at the Brooklyn Vocational School in 1902.

A banquet in 1925 marks the 15th anniversary of the founding of the Progressive Samborer landsmanshaft.

Members of the San Antonio, Texas, chapter of the Council of Jewish Women with books collected for the public library.

ASSOCIATIONS

The Jewish community created many organizations to make life in America easier. Some of the most successful were the landsmanshaften, *societies of people from the same area in the homeland. They provided insurance for members and social comfort. In New York City the larger ones had their own cafes where they regularly socialized. The* Jewish Daily Forward *of January 17, 1914, commented:*

Vilna, Minsk, Berditchev, Homl. Each of these cities and towns is represented by New York cafes. Odessa politics, Vilna diplomacy are reflected through representatives of these places back home who dispatch representatives to the East Side basement parliament....

One feels at home in these *landsleit* cafes. The outside is shabby but inside it's clean and tidy, the floor covered by sawdust just as in Europe. White tablecloths are on the tables, and the visiting Vilner feels that his own mother is about to arrive with a Sabbath smile and the candlesticks as she's about to bless the candles. A peaceful stillness spreads about the room. Minsk is Minsk and Vilna is Vilna. The ocean and America notwithstanding, a familiar plate of barley soup in the basement of Vilna, Volkoviski, Shavel, or Kurenitz brings you back home....

On the windows of the various Russian cafes there's an added decoration: "Russian spoken here." Your reporter wanted to know if such signs indeed draw Russian clientele. Said the proprietor, "We attract intellectual *landsleit*. It's a treat to be given both a meal and the chance to converse in Russian."

Jewish Americans collected funds and provided volunteer workers for countless Jewish charitable organizations. May Weisser, born on the Lower East Side of New York in 1900, described in her autobiography how her immigrant parents helped found the Hebrew National Orphan Home.

The Orthodox Jews collected funds for hospitals and homes for the aged, and for orphanages where kosher food could be served and other religious customs of their forefathers observed. The Hebrew Immigrant Aid Society, Beth Israel Hospital, and the Home of the Daughters of Jacob were among many East Side institutions that were to become famous.

Bessarabia, a Rumanian-speaking province of Russia, was the birthplace of my parents. The Bessarabian Verband Association was composed of many lodges and societies, organized by immigrants from the little towns of Bessarabia.

There was a crying need for a home where orphan boys,

between the ages of six and fourteen, could be raised in the Orthodox tenets of the Faith, and the Bessarabian Verband started the organization which was to become the Hebrew National Orphan Home.

My parents were among the founders and much of their activity took place in our home. My mother helped organize the first Ladies Auxiliary and my sisters Sally and Minnie started the Young Folks Auxiliary.

The Verband purchased and renovated a fine brownstone house for the orphans at 37 East 7th Street, between First and Second Avenues, on the lower East Side....

The official opening was scheduled for June 7, 1914, with a celebration to last an entire week. This would be a fund-raising event.

For several months, the Board and Auxiliaries had been selling raffle tickets and collecting thousands of prizes from merchants and manufacturers. Tickets of admission to the celebration were fifty cents each and entitled the owner to a prize, according to his luck when he pulled a number.

I volunteered my services and at the age of 14 I started at the beginning of June to work in the Home.

Hadassah was founded by Henrietta Szold in 1912 as a women's group dedicated to the health care of the Jews in Palestine. It eventually became the Women's Zionist Organization of America. Eli Evans remembered his mother and grandmother's dedication to the Zionist movement. His grandmother started the first Hadassah chapter in North Carolina.

Hadassah had been her life from her early twenties. My grandmother Jennie wanted to see Palestine before she died, so in 1933, Dad scraped together the money for Jennie, her limp from childhood polio growing worse with age, to see the promised land with her daughter. The experience fired my mother's idealism and her sense of mission, and from then on she devoted all of her emotional and physical energy to Israel through Hadassah. For years she was president of the Durham chapter as well as of the seaboard region, and she represented the South on the National Board. Year in and year out, she would argue the gritty details for the annual donor affair; battle with the Federation [of Jewish Philanthropies, successor to the United Hebrew Charities] when the men wanted to cut down on the percentage contribution to Israel [out of the funds collected] because of local needs; and sit on the telephone for hours and hours squeezing ads out of local gentile businesses for the Hadassah yearbook, complaining of their reluctance to my father, who would make it a point at the next Kiwanis Club luncheon to tell the president of Montgomery-Aldridge Tire Company that he really ought to buy a larger ad because "those women treat that yearbook like their shopping Bible."

"Hello, Mr. Aldridge, this is Mrs. E. J. Evans. We're trying to save the children again this year...." I honestly felt that she built the Hadassah hospital, brick by brick, right at that phone on the breakfast table.

Henrietta Szold

The daughter of a rabbi, Henrietta Szold was born in Baltimore in 1860. Her parents, immigrants from Hungary, had eight children, all of them girls. Henrietta's father treated her as a son, encouraging her to study the Torah and the Talmud. After his death in 1902 she said the kaddish, or prayer of mourning, for him in the synagogue—traditionally the responsibility of a Jewish eldest son or male kinsman.

After graduating from high school, Szold became a teacher in a private school and also taught at the religious school in the synagogue where her father was rabbi. When Jewish refugees from Russia began to arrive in Baltimore in the 1880s, she opened a night school where they could learn English. In 1898, she became editor of the Jewish Publication Society, which translated Jewish classics into English.

In 1909, Szold traveled to Palestine, a journey that changed her life. The miserable living conditions of the Jewish population there shocked her. After returning to the United States, in 1912 she founded the first chapter of the Women's Zionist Organization of America. Known as Hadassah (the Hebrew name of Esther, the Jewish queen of Persia who saved her people from destruction), the organization attracted many Jewish American women who sought an active role in religious activities.

Until her death, Szold worked tirelessly on behalf of Hadassah's many activities. During World War I, Hadassah sent medical personnel to war-torn Palestine, offering aid to Arabs as well as Jews. Later, under Szold's direction, Hadassah established health centers and schools in Palestine. After Hitler came to power in Germany in 1933, Szold founded Youth Aliyah, which took refugee children from Nazi Germany to Palestine. Her energy awed those who were much younger; she often worked 20-hour days when she was well over 70, and even in her 80s rested only on the Sabbath.

In February 1945, Szold died in Jerusalem's Hadassah Hebrew University Hospital, which she had helped to found. She was buried in the Jewish cemetery on the Mount of Olives.

Three generations of a Jewish American family light Hanukkah candles: Aron and Manette Berlinger, their daughter Gabrielle, and Manette's parents, Harry and Pola Reinitz.

CHAPTER SIX

PART OF AMERICA

lthough Jewish Americans make up only about 3 percent of the total population of the United States, their achievements have touched the lives of all their fellow citizens. In the 1960s Albert Sabin and Jonas Salk developed the vaccines that wiped out polio, a crippling disease that formerly afflicted many children. Edwin Land invented the Polaroid camera, which millions of Americans have used to make instant pictures of family events. Steven Spielberg directed the two most popular movies of all time—*E.T.* and *Jurassic Park*—and won an Academy Award for best director in 1994 for *Schindler's List,* a riveting story of Jewish survival during the Holocaust.

The Jewish immigrants who fled Europe during the 1930s to escape the Holocaust provided a wealth of talent to their adopted country. One of the best known is Albert Einstein, the German-born genius whose theories revolutionized the science of physics. At Einstein's urging, President Franklin Roosevelt began the program to develop an atomic bomb during World War II. Many other Jewish scientists who were refugees from Hitler's Europe contributed to the development of the weapon that

made the United States the world's strongest military power.

Since the end of World War II, a higher percentage of Jewish American students have attended college than any other American group. By some estimates as many as 20 percent of all American lawyers and physicians are Jewish; nearly the same percentage of college professors is Jewish.

Jewish Americans have made some of their greatest achievements in the field of communications. Journalism's most coveted honor, the Pulitzer Prize, is named after German Jewish immigrant Joseph Pulitzer, who published the *St. Louis Post-Dispatch* and the *New York World* between 1878 and his death in 1911. The *New York Times,* today the nation's leading newspaper, is owned by the Sulzberger family—descendants of Adolph S. Ochs, the son of an immigrant who purchased what was then a failing newspaper in 1896.

The U.S. motion picture industry was virtually created by Jewish American immigrants. Louis B. Mayer, born in the Russian Pale in 1885, moved with his family to Canada. Supposedly, young Louis earned his first dollar by collecting scrap metal when he was only eight. Moving to the United States as a young man, he opened a nickelodeon, where customers paid an

admission price of five cents to view moving pictures through the eyepiece of a crank-operated machine. It was only a short time before he began to produce his own movies. Samuel Goldwyn (born in Poland as Schmuel Gelbfisz) came to America in 1895 as a 13-year-old orphan. After finding work as a glove salesman, he began to manufacture gloves himself. In 1913 he financed his first movie. The companies founded by Mayer and Goldwyn later merged into what is today MGM (Metro-Goldwyn-Mayer).

Harry Cohn, founder of Columbia Pictures; Adolph Zukor, who started Paramount Pictures; Darryl F. Zanuck and Joseph Schenck, whose company later became known as Twentieth Century-Fox; and the Warner Brothers—Jack, Harry, Sam, and Albert—are among the other Jewish Americans who created the motion picture industry.

In time, radio and television reached even larger audiences than the movies—and these media also resulted from the work of Jewish Americans. In 1915, Russian-born immigrant David Sarnoff, a telegraph operator for the Marconi Wireless Telegraph Company in New York, suggested that the company expand its business by selling home radio sets and broadcasting music programs. His plan was the beginning of an industry that reaches into practically every American household. In 1926, Sarnoff started the first nationwide radio network, the National Broadcasting Company (NBC).

During the 1930s, Sarnoff financed the development of television. The first successful broadcast, in fuzzy black-and-white, took place in 1939. At Sarnoff's death in 1971, the television industry he created had become the most popular form of entertainment in the United States.

William S. Paley, who became president of the Columbia Broadcasting System (CBS) in 1928, and Leonard Goldenson, who became chairman of the American Broadcasting Company (ABC) in 1953, were two other Jewish American pioneers in broadcast media.

Jewish American composers, entertainers, and writers have had an enormous influence on American culture. Irving Berlin (born in Russia in 1888 as Israel Baline) came to America with his parents at the age of four. He became one of the most popular American composers of the 20th century, writing more than 1,000 songs, such as "Alexander's Ragtime Band," "There's No Business Like Show Business," "White Christmas," and "God Bless America."

George Gershwin, born in New York in 1898 of Russian Jewish parents, wrote many musical comedies with his brother Ira, including *Of Thee I Sing* (1931), the first

musical to win a Pulitzer Prize. George Gershwin made a lasting mark on American music with his works, which combined American jazz with the European classical tradition. His *Rhapsody in Blue,* first performed in 1924, startled the music world with its originality. Before his tragically early death at age 39, Gershwin also wrote *An American in Paris* and the opera *Porgy and Bess.*

The youngest child at the table asks the traditional four questions at a seder dinner in Los Angeles.

Jewish Americans' contributions to stage music have continued through the work of such composer-writer teams as Richard Rodgers and Oscar Hammerstein II, creators of *Oklahoma!, The King and I,* and *South Pacific.* Alan Jay Lerner and Frederick Loewe, who collaborated on several musicals and screenplays, wrote *My Fair Lady,* one of the most successful musicals of all time.

From the 1950s to his death in 1990, Leonard Bernstein carried on the work of popularizing classical music through his television programs with the New York

Philharmonic Orchestra. Bernstein also composed classical music, but his best-known work is the Broadway musical *West Side Story.*

Stephen Sondheim, who studied songwriting under Hammerstein and wrote the lyrics for Bernstein's *West Side Story,* is today one of the stars of Broadway musical theater, with many hits for which he wrote both music and lyrics.

The works of Jewish American playwrights have often explored serious themes. In the depression years of the 1930s, Clifford Odets wrote several plays about the struggles of working-class Americans. Arthur Miller won the Pulitzer Prize in 1949 for *Death of a Salesman,* which made a tragic hero of Willy Loman, a man regarded as a failure by everyone but his sons.

American theater has also been enriched by the talents of such comic playwrights as George S. Kaufman and Moss Hart, who wrote *You Can't Take It with You* and *The Man Who Came to Dinner* in the 1930s. Neil Simon's unbroken record of hit comedies began with *Come Blow Your Horn* in 1961 and continues today. Simon now has a Broadway theater named after him—the only time a living playwright has been so honored.

Jewish American entertainers have delighted audiences in all the forms of mass media. Comedians such as Jack Benny, Milton Berle, and Jerry Lewis starred in radio, television, and the movies. Two of the top TV programs of the 1990s, *Roseanne* and *Seinfeld,* are named after their Jewish American creators. Barbra Streisand, Billy Joel, and Bob Dylan are among the most popular Jewish American recording artists.

The novels and stories of such Jewish American writers as Bernard Malamud, E. L. Doctorow, Norman Mailer, J. D. Salinger, Grace Paley, Judith Krantz, Leon Uris, Philip Roth, and Nobel Prize winner Saul Bellow have become best-sellers. The books of Judy Blume and Maurice Sendak have delighted millions of young Americans.

Isaac Bashevis Singer—whose works re-create the world of Jewish communities in his native Poland—was awarded the Nobel Prize in 1978. He delivered his acceptance speech in Yiddish, the language in which he first wrote his many novels and stories before they were translated into English.

All of these successes have brought Jews into the mainstream of American life and culture—so much so that some Jewish Americans worry that assimilation, or the absorption of Jews into secular society, would result in the loss of Jewish identity. As prosperous Jews moved out of their old inner-city neighborhoods into suburbs after 1945, some established new synagogues as a focus for the community. Orthodox Judaism lost many adherents to the Conservative and Reform forms of Judaism. Between 1970 and 1990, the percentage of Orthodox Jews among Jewish Americans

declined from 11 percent to 7 percent. In 1990, Reform Jews made up 38 percent of the population, and Conservative Jews were 35 percent.

Intermarriage between Jews and non-Jews has become a cause for concern among the Jewish American community. A population survey conducted by the Council of Jewish Federations in the early 1990s showed that 52 percent of

A group of children in Camden, New Jersey, celebrates the founding of Israel in 1948.

Jews who had married in the last five years chose a non-Jew as a spouse. The same survey showed that 72 percent of mixed-marriage couples were raising their children outside the Jewish faith. These figures caused dismay because they seemed to forecast an inevitable decline in Amerian Judaism.

In fact, the number of Jewish Americans has remained steady at about 6 million since 1970. About 1.1 million of these are secular Jews, who do not practice any form of Judaism. However, even among the majority who maintained a religious identity, only

about 30 percent were members of a synagogue.

In chapters of Hillel, an organization of Jewish college students, in such pulications as *Commentary* and *Tikkun,* and in the homes of many Jewish Americans, the question "What does it mean to be a Jew?" is discussed and debated. Many of the youngest generation of American Jews are finding that the ethical values of Judaism remain as relevant today as they were when Moses came down from Mount Sinai with the Ten Commandments more than 3,000 years ago.

The establishment of the state of Israel in 1948 and attacks on Israel by its Arab neighbors have brought an outpouring of support from American Jews, both secular and religious. The plight of persecuted Soviet Jews also provided a unifying element that reminded many Jewish Americans of their identity as part of the worldwide community of Jews. To some extent, American Judaism has experienced a revival of fervor by the arrival of about 225,000 Jewish immigrants from Israel and the Soviet Union since 1970.

By contrast, only a small number of American Jews have left the United States to settle in Israel. The vast majority of American Jews are contented with life in the country that has sheltered their ancestors from 1654 to the present day. They consider themselves as American as the members of any other immigrant group—and their success and acceptance in all areas of American life prove that to be true.

Beverly Sills retired from her long and successful career as an opera singer to become general director of the New York City Opera in 1980. James Levine, artistic director of New York's Metropolitan Opera, has also been a guest conductor for orchestras around the world.

In the 1950s, comedian Milton Berle was known as Mr. Television. His Texaco Star Theater was the most popular program of the decade, a time when most American families bought their first TV set.

ENTERTAINMENT

After the arrival of eastern European immigrants, the Lower East Side of New York blossomed with theaters and dance halls. Some of the most successful entertainers in the United States first performed there. Ed Renard recalled how he entered show business with the comedian George Burns around 1910.

You couldn't exactly call my first stage appearance a success. I was 15 and I got into an amateur night on the Bowery. They gave me the hook before I could open up my mouth, but that didn't discourage me. I was born on Second Avenue and Sixth Street and the only recreation we had was going to dance halls. We went to seven dances a week and one matinee Saturday. Naturally, we were all good ballroom dancers. So the first venture we had was a ballroom-dancing act with a girl from school—then I had a dancing school with George Burns. We had mostly foreigners that wanted to learn how to dance; the girls would sit on one side of the hall and the boys on the other side. We used to go and give exhibitions for dancers for [the prize of] a cup. Burns would be the judge, so I won the cup. Then I would be the judge, so Burns won the cup.

Then I had an act with Burns. My name at that time was Fields. We went to Brooklyn for the matinee and the manager takes one look at us and closes us. About five months later I decide to do a single so I book myself into the same house under a different name. In the morning, the manager is watching the rehearsal from the back and he comes down the aisle. "Weren't you here six months ago?" "No, not me." "Wasn't your name Fields?" "No, Renard." He looks blank for a minute but goes back, and I start singing my number. All of a sudden he rushes down the aisle. "Get out, Fields." That was that.

The Catskill resorts, in the mountains about 100 miles northwest of New York City, became a popular vacation spot for Jewish American families. Many of the resorts became showcases for talented entertainers. Milton Kutsher, the owner of a popular Catskill resort, spoke to interviewers in 1978 about his family's business.

My father and uncle came to the Lower East Side from Austria in 1903. My father was 17, my uncle 27. From working fifteen to sixteen hours a day, six days a week, my uncle's health began to deteriorate. The doctors told him it would be smart to get out of New York, so he persuaded my father to come out here and buy a farm. Everyone thought they were crazy, but they went ahead anyway and bought a farmhouse with two hundred acres of surrounding land. In order to make ends meet, they began taking boarders in the summer, mostly people they knew from the Lower East Side....

Today people expect to be entertained, but when people know entertainment isn't provided they provide it for themselves. In the old days parents played cards and sat in the sun, children fooled around the fields, couples took walks along the country roads. On Friday night and Saturday night, in the same room, my uncle told jokes and danced the kazatska. That was the entertainment. People then didn't expect like people expect today. These were poor Jews who paid as little as five dollars a week for a bed and three meals a day. All they really wanted was the good food and the fresh air.

The Borscht Belt, as the Catskill resorts became known after the popular Russian beet soup served there, was a training ground for many Jewish comedians. Henny Youngman described his experiences there during the 1920s.

I was, in a word, a *tummler.* In Yiddish, this word means "noise." And that definition, basically, was the actual job description. *Noise.* My charge was to keep people busy and happy and not thinking about how crappy the food or the rooms were at the resort. If the guests are laughing, went the owner's philosophy, then they're not complaining or checking out.

Now this probably doesn't sound like too dignified a job. Actually, the professional *tummler* is a Jewish tradition that dates back to the Middle Ages. Back then there was a guy named a *badchen* whose job it was to run around at weddings making lots of slapstick noise. It's a sacred commandment to be joyous at weddings, and the *badchen*'s job was to do whatever was necessary to keep everybody giggling.

At the Swan Lake Inn, doing whatever was necessary meant a *tummler* also had to be an emcee, scenic designer, electrician, and sometimes a busboy. After shows, he had to hang around and schmooze up [talk with] the guests.... Then there was our most sacred duty—trying to fix up unattached men and women....

From a *tummler*'s perspective, the worst thing that could ever happen was for a drop of rain to fall upon his guests. Whenever it rained, you see, the patrons would tramp back into the main lodge to angrily bray and complain all the way until the next meal.

This was my audience. Talk about working a rough room. But to learn how to make these tough, smart...vacationers from the city laugh was the best comedy trade school a guy could have wanted.

Just look at a partial list of borscht-belt *tummlers* who made it to the big time: Danny Kaye, Jan Peerce, Jan Murray, Tony Curtis, Jerry Lewis, Red Buttons, Phil Silvers, Moss Hart, Jack Albertson, Joey Adams, Jack Carter, and Phil Foster.

Barbra Streisand

Born in Brooklyn in 1942, Barbra Streisand was a shy, unpopular girl who yearned for a career as an actress. She resisted her mother's advice to take typing and shorthand in school "just in case." When she was 19, Streisand entered a talent contest and won $50 and a contract to sing in a nightclub.

Though Streisand had no formal training as a singer, her style entranced audiences and music critics. Pop music composer Jule Styne wrote, "Barbra makes each song sound like a well-written three-act play performed stunningly in three minutes."

In 1962, a Broadway producer cast Streisand in a musical comedy. Her performance brought many offers from TV show producers and record company executives. *The Barbra Streisand Album,* released in 1963, hit the top of the music charts. Two more albums soon followed.

The following year, she took the starring role in the Broadway musical *Funny Girl.* Playing Fanny Brice, a Jewish American singer and actress, Streisand was a smash success. In 1968, she repeated the role in a movie that won her an Academy Award for best actress. The "ugly duckling," as she once described herself, had reached the heights of show business at the age of 26.

Since then, Streisand has continually expanded her talents. In 1976, she coauthored the Academy Award–winning song "Evergreen" for the movie *A Star Is Born,* which she produced and starred in. In 1983, she produced and directed *Yentl,* in which she played an Orthodox Jewish girl who disguised herself as a boy in order to enter rabbinical school. She also took dramatic roles in several movies.

In 1994, for the first time in 20 years, Streisand appeared in a series of live concerts. At age 52, she demonstrated that she had not lost her ability to thrill audiences with song.

Leonard Bernstein

On November 14, 1943, Leonard Bernstein received an urgent phone call. The renowned conductor Bruno Walter was too ill to lead the New York Philharmonic orchestra in a concert that night. Bernstein, the assistant conductor, would have to take his place. Only 25 and virtually unknown to the music world, Bernstein gave an astounding performance, although he had had no time for rehearsals.

That was the beginning of a career that made Bernstein the best-known figure in American classical music. He was born in 1918 in Lawrence, Massachusetts, the son of Russian immigrants. His talent for music appeared when he was 10, after a relative lent the family an old piano. Though his father opposed his decision to pursue a career in music, Bernstein persisted in following his dream.

After his 1943 conducting debut, Bernstein accepted many offers to conduct orchestras throughout the United States and Europe. From 1958 to 1969, he served as conductor and musical director of the New York Philharmonic. In the 1950s and 1960s, Bernstein brought classical music to a wider audience by introducing a series of nationally televised concerts for young people. He left the Philharmonic in 1969 to devote his time to composing.

Bernstein's talent was wide-ranging. He wrote the music for several Broadway musicals, including *West Side Story*. He composed ballets, an opera, and music for films such as *On the Waterfront* and Walt Disney's *Peter Pan*. His many classical works were as diverse as the symphony *Kaddish* (based on the Jewish prayer for the dead) and the *Mass* performed at the opening of the John F. Kennedy Center in Washington, D.C. At his death in 1990, Bernstein left a musical legacy of recordings and compositions that will keep his memory alive.

Abe Burrows, an author, producer, and director, knew the movie producer Samuel Goldwyn. He recalled:

Legendary" is one of the most misused words in our language, and rather stale besides, but it really fitted Sam Goldwyn. He deserved it because at least half the stories about him were legends made up by press agents and people who claimed to know him and usually didn't. A lot of the fake stories about Sam made him sound silly. He was not silly. He was a bright, tough guy with a great love for films. And he made only films he personally liked. A few of them were ordinary, but most of them were excellent. At any rate, all of them were pictures he personally chose to do, wanted to do, and loved to make. This is now a very rare thing in Hollywood. Those old picturemakers—Goldwyn, Cohn, Zanuck, Mayer and Warner—all had one thing in common: they really liked the movies they made. They went by their own taste and judgment. This often led to ordinary, routine films, but just as often it led to some pretty good ones. Today the picturemakers try to guess what the public will like, and that frequently leads to dull imitations of dull imitations. Sam Goldwyn was special. In a corporate motion-picture world he was a solo performer. If the public didn't agree with his taste, it was their fault.

Jack Benny became one of America's best-loved comedians through his shows on radio and television. Born Benjamin Kubelsky in Illinois in 1894, Benny recalled that the success of the Jewish musical prodigy Mischa Elman made his own mother force him to take violin lessons.

I loved the violin, but I hated practicing.... When Mama went over to help in the store, I stopped practicing. I'd watch the boats. I'd watch the people by the docks. I'd fall into a trance and dream of running away to faroff countries. I would try to keep an eye out for Mama, crossing the street. She was a tall, slender, beautiful woman with sad blue eyes and long dark hair. Usually she was sweet and gentle and patient. Sometimes, seemingly for no reason, she would fall into a depression and be bitter for days and sometimes she would get violently angry. I often aroused her anger. I would get so dreamy that I would forget to watch out for Mama returning home to make supper. She'd come into the parlor and see me with the fiddle on my lap and the bow hanging down on the floor.

"Benny, what are you doing?"

"I don't know, Ma."

"Why ain't you practicing?"

"I finished already," I lied.

"It's only five o'clock."

"I don't wanna practice. I don't wanna be a musician. I can't help it, Mama," I said, sighing.

"Look at Mischa Elman. He's your age and already he's famous. All over the world people know about Mischa Elman.

And why? From working hard. From sticking. You got a talent like a Mischa Elman only you must practice to bring it out."

"Yes, Mama."...

There is a saying that coming events cast their shadows before them. My parents and I saw the shadows and not the events. I'm told that when I was three years old I liked to get a smile out of people by reciting poems and singing nursery rhymes. My best audience was Grandma Sachs and Papa's sister, Aunt Clara. I would collect all the chairs and put them in rows in the parlor. Then I would put on a little show. Sometimes I played the piano and later, when I was learning to play the fiddle, I added a few violin solos. When I was eight years old I performed at the Saturday children's matinees at the Phoenix Opera House. I would be dressed in velvet knickerbockers, a white silk shirt and a black Windsor tie. Grandma thought I was adorable. At one concert I played a medley of Stephen Foster songs with piano accompaniment.

"You should be proud of Benny," Grandma said.

"He don't practice," Mama said. "Without practicing, he'll be a nothing."

"You'll see," Grandma prophesied.

"What'll I see? From this he's making a living? 'Old Black Joe'? 'Way Down Upon a River'? This is music! He ain't fit to carry Mischa Elman's rosin."

"You'll see," was Grandma's answer.

"I should live so long," Mama would say, sighing.

Poor Mama. She didn't live so long. She died of cancer in 1917 when she was 47 and I was 23. In the meantime I was a bitter disappointment—a cheap fiddle act in vaudeville and she never came to see me because she thought show business was immoral.

Jerry Seinfeld, at left, is the latest in a long line of popular Jewish American comedians. On his top-rated weekly television show, Seinfeld creates humor from everyday situations.

Steven Spielberg

The first movie Steven Spielberg ever saw was *The Greatest Show on Earth,* a spectacular circus movie. Spielberg was only five, and his father worried that he might be too young for such excitement. He told Steven, "It's going to be bigger than you, but that's all right. The people in it are going to be up on a screen and they can't get out at you." But as Spielberg later recalled, "There they were up on that screen *and they were getting out at me.* I guess ever since then I've wanted to try to involve the audience as much as I can."

Spielberg has succeeded as few people in the movie business ever have. He started by using his father's home-movie camera to make horror films starring his three younger sisters. In 1969, while a college student, he made a 22-minute film called *Amblin'* about two hitchhikers. After the film won awards at the Venice and Atlanta film festivals, a studio signed him to make TV movies.

Five years later, Spielberg directed his first feature film, *The Sugarland Express.* Despite praise from movie critics, it flopped at the box office. However, his next project was the movie version of the best-selling novel *Jaws.* During the filming, Spielberg was almost fired because he went far over budget. But in the first month after the movie's release, ticket sales exceeded $60 million—almost 10 times what the movie had cost.

In 1977, Spielberg followed that success with *Close Encounters of the Third Kind,* an eerie movie about aliens visiting the earth. Five years later, Spielberg turned the alien into a lovable creature called *E.T.,* in what became the highest-grossing movie of all time. Spielberg's successes continued with the Indiana Jones movies and *Jurassic Park.* But his greatest triumph came in 1994 with *Schindler's List,* a harrowing movie about the Holocaust. For the first time in his brilliant career, Spielberg won the Academy Award for best director.

Today, Spielberg heads his own film production company, called Amblin Entertainment, which finances independent filmmakers. In 1994, with David Geffen and Jeffrey Katzenberg, he formed a new company that will produce films for theaters and television as well as for CD and home video distribution.

In 1973, two Jewish immigrants from the Soviet Union are reunited at Kennedy airport in New York. The daughter, at left, immigrated earlier and waited anxiously for her mother to receive an exit visa.

NEW COMMUNITIES

Jewish immigrants have continued to arrive in the United States since the end of World War II in 1945. They bring their own traditions that contribute to the varied community of Jewish Americans.

Tilly Stimler, who was born in Romania in 1930, survived the concentration camps of the Holocaust. She married a fellow concentration-camp survivor in Belgium after the war. They came to the United States in 1952 with the help of the Hebrew Immigrant Aid Society (HIAS).

I had a brother here, and distant relatives and friends. But still it took some time getting used to this place. We lived in Newark [New Jersey] for a short while and then moved to the Bronx. My husband went to work in a leather-goods shop, and we adapted well. Later on someone in the family suggested that my husband try to become a butcher and go into business for himself. He agreed, and after working a long time he was able to open his own store in West Orange [New Jersey]....

I'm proud to say that my husband and I brought up two well-adjusted children. My son was born in 1952 and has a wife and child and lives in New York. He is very bright; he finished college when he was nineteen and then he took Talmudic studies. He's dedicated to studying the Talmud. My daughter lives in Baltimore, is married and has twins.

As I look back now, I really think that being very religious is the most important thing. It helps you to understand that there's a purpose in life. Even if you go through hardships, you are able to make it.

I remember my son asking me once, "Mommy, if the camps were so bad, how did you survive?" And my only answer was, and has always been, "For some reason, God wanted me to live."

Hasidism is a movement within Judaism that arose in Poland in the 18th century. Its founders stressed the importance of an emotional acceptance of God, in contrast to the scholarly study of Judaic law. Adherents of the movement, called Hasidim, express their devotion with ecstatic prayer that includes dancing and singing. Hadsidic men wear black suits and broad-brimmed hats.

The Holocaust destroyed most of the Hasidic communities that thrived in Europe before World War II. Survivors emigrated to neighborhoods in Brooklyn, New York, where small numbers of Hasidim had lived since the early 20th century. In recent years, Hasidim have established communities in upstate New York as well. The chief figure in each Hasidic community is the rebbe, or

At a Hasidic wedding, the bride's face is covered throughout the ceremony. Here, the mother guides her daughter's arm as the groom places a ring on her finger.

chief rabbi. Rabbi Meyer Weberman, rebbe of the M'lochim community in upstate New York, explains his role.

A rabbi is somebody who has studied more law than other people. When there's a question of what to do I'm able to tell them. Also I can hold sermons, with the help of God, to show them what I believe is the right thing to do. That's as far as it goes. I can convey to them what I feel is right, but I don't profess that I can perceive and that I can expect to know what they actually need.

The Rebbe is someone who recognizes the functions of the soul. He can direct a person, help him, with wisdom and prayer, to control himself and to guide him in the proper way. The Rebbe can anticipate the problems that everybody encounters in everyday life. He counsels him how to serve his Creator during the course of prayer, the study of Talmud, performing mitzvot [acts of merit]. That's what a Rebbe means.

Ties between the Jewish communities in the United States and Israel are strong. Sometimes Jews from Israel come to the United States in order to further their studies and then become citizens. Such was the case of Israeli Ralph Mishan, who immigrated in 1960.

I [got] a diploma in engineering [and] did my army service in Israel. I came to the United States to continue my studies at Columbia University.... I concluded my master's degree in 1961.

According to United States law I was entitled to 18 months of practical training in my profession before returning to my country. I found work as a graduate engineer [at] Swingline Corporation; they make staples and staplers. Apparently I was something good from their point of view.... When I came to ask permission to extend my stay as a foreign student, they said, "...Why don't you take immigrant status? If you choose to return to your country, you can still do so. But hold on to the immigrant status and then you won't have to get...extensions every six months."

I said, "Fine, let's go ahead and do it." I became a permanent resident and from then on it was just a matter of five years and I became a citizen.

Jews from the Soviet Union eagerly sought to emigrate to the United States after the 1960s. Zhanna Drantyev, who emigrated with her husband in the 1980s, told an interviewer about her impressions of her adopted country.

When I left Russia, for the first time I realized how isolated we were in the USSR. The fashion and style magazines here were so incredibly creative. I like to see the people on the street with their spiked hair and strange clothes. I love the freedom people have to express themselves. Although freedom also means more crime and offensive behavior, I've lived with censorship and the price is too high. The feeling of freedom that you feel on the streets here is a very special and valuable treasure.

The Lubavitcher sect of Hasidic Jews has its world headquarters in Brooklyn, New York. Inside the building, this man has put on phylacteries to say prayers. The boxes on his forehead and left arm contain passages from the Bible. Customarily, Orthodox Jews stand while praying.

In 1972, Sally Jane Preisand was ordained by Hebrew Union College–Jewish Institute of Religion in Cincinnati. She became the first female rabbi in the United States.

Simchas Torah is the day on which the yearly cycle of the reading of the Torah ends and begins again. The scrolls, adorned with silver breastplates and crowns, are removed from the ark in the synagogue and carried in a joyful procession. Here, in a Milwaukee celebration, a scroll is carried through the streets.

LINKING OLD AND NEW TRADITIONS

Many Jewish Americans today experience a desire for a deeper sense of Jewishness in their lives. Paul Cowan described his feelings in his 1982 autobiography.

For more than four years now, I have been embarked on a wondrous, confusing voyage through time and culture. Until 1976 when I was 36, I had always identified myself as an American Jew. Now I am an American and a Jew. I live at once in the years 1982 and 5743, the Jewish year in which I am publishing this book. I am Paul Cowan, the New York-bred son of Louis Cowan and Pauline Spiegel Cowan, Chicago-born, very American, very successful parents; and I am Saul Cohen, the descendant of rabbis in Germany and Lithuania. I am the grandson of Modie Spiegel, a mail-order magnate, who was born a Reform Jew, became a Christian Scientist, and died in his spacious house in the wealthy Gentile suburb of Kenilworth, Illinois, with a picture of Jesus Christ in his breast pocket; and of Jacob Cohen, a used-cement-bag dealer from Chicago, an Orthodox Jew, who lost everything he had—his wife, his son, his business, his self-esteem—except for the superstition-tinged faith that gave moments of structure and meaning to his last, lonely years.

As a child, growing up on Manhattan's East Side, I lived among Jewish WASPs [white Anglo-Saxon Protestants]. My father, an only child, had changed his name from Cohen to Cowan when he was twenty-one. He was so guarded about his youth that he never let my brothers or sisters or me meet any of his father's relatives. I always thought of myself as a Cowan—the Welsh word for stonecutter—not a Cohen—a member of the Jewish priestly caste. My family celebrated Christmas and always gathered for an Easter dinner of ham and sweet potatoes…. In those years, I barely knew what a Passover seder was. I didn't know anyone who practiced archaic customs such as keeping kosher or lighting candles on Friday night. Neither my parents nor I ever mentioned the possibility of a bar mitzvah. In 1965, I fell in love with Rachel Brown, a New England Protestant whose ancestors came here in the 17th century. It didn't matter in the least bit to her—or to me—that we were an interfaith marriage.

Now, at 42, I care more about Jewish holidays I'd never heard of back then, Shavuot or Simchat Torah, than about Christmas or Easter. In 1980, fifteen years after we were married, Rachel converted to Judaism, and is now program director of Ansche Chesed, a neighborhood synagogue we are trying to revitalize. Our family lights Friday night candles, and neither

Rachel nor I work on the Sabbath. Since 1974, our children, Lisa and Mamu, have gone to the Havurah School, a once-a-week Jewish school we started, and at fourteen and twelve they're more familiar with the Torah than I was five years ago. They were very thoughtful children, who have witnessed the changes in our family's life and are somewhat bemused and ambivalent about them. There is no telling whether they'll follow the path we have chosen. But that is true of all children. This past September, Lisa undertook the difficult task of learning her bat mitzvah at Ansche Chesed. That day I was as happy as I've ever been in my life.

Young Jewish Americans are rediscovering their ancient roots. Susan C. Grossman, born in 1955, was a member of the first class of women accepted into the rabbinical study program at the Jewish Theological Seminary (JTS). Ordained in 1989, she serves as rabbi of Genesis Agudas Achim congregation in Tuckahoe, New York. Grossman described the path that led her to become a rabbi.

I did not receive any formal Jewish education when I was a child, although I was raised to believe in God and support the state of Israel. We were an average Jewish family, celebrating the Passover *seder*, lighting the *menorah*, and eating *hamentaschen* [triangular shaped cookies] on Purim. As part of my 1970s pilgrimage to San Francisco, ostensibly as a visiting student to study television for a semester at San Francisco State, I met Shlomo Carlbach and at his House of Love and Prayer there began to learn about Jewish observance. Several years of living in various upper New York State cities, on first jobs, allowed me to study with Conservative and Lubavitch [a Hasidic sect] rabbis. When I finally came to New York to study more seriously, I was already thinking of rabbinical school, but found that JTS was not open to women. I began studying for a masters in Judaic studies at Brooklyn College, and working in

Rabbi Herbert G. Panich of Congregation Beth Israel in Milwaukee sounds the shofar, or ram's horn, at a demonstration in support of Soviet Jews in 1971.

As an old man, American Rabbi Stephen S. Wise, who worked actively to create a Jewish state, wrote: "I thank God it was given to me to live till that glorious day of May 14, 1948, when out of the centuries of persecution, of prayer and hope and labor, the prophecy of Theodor Herzl was at last fulfilled." Because Rabbi Wise was too frail to travel, he never saw Israel. He died the following year.

In a religious school in Cincinnati, young Jewish boys learn Hebrew so that they will be able to read the Torah.

the Jewish community during the day, hoping to become a scholar and communal leader if I could not become a rabbi since I have a deep seated feeling that God wants me to be working in the Jewish community.

In Judaism, Hanukkah is the eight-day Feast of Lights that sometimes falls in December. Faye Moskowitz, a teacher, recalled that when she was growing up, her gentile friends called Hanukkah "Jewish Christmas." Indeed, the ever-present reminders of Christmas often made the Jewish children feel like outsiders. However, when her family moved to a Jewish neighborhood in Detroit, Michigan, Faye Moskowitz felt more comfortable with her own tradition.

I was old enough to accept Christmas as a holiday other people celebrated. Chanukah was our winter holiday, not a substitute at all, but a minor-league festival that paled before Passover, Rosh Hashanah, and Yom Kippur. All the cousins gathered at our grandparents' house where we lined up to get Chanukah gelt ["gold," or money presents] from the uncles: quarters and half dollars, and dollar bills, perhaps, for the older children. Mostly we ran around a lot, got very flushed, and ate latkes [potato pancakes], plenty of them....

My aunts sucked in their bellies as they elbowed past one another in and out of Bobbe's [Yiddish for "grandmother"] tiny kitchen, from which they pulled a seemingly endless array of delicious dishes as if from a magician's opera hat: platters of bagels slathered with cream cheese, smoked fish with skins of iridescent gold, pickled herring, thick slices of Bermuda onion strong enough to prompt a double-dare, boiled potatoes with their red jackets on, wallowing in butter. Best of all were the crisp potato latkes, hot from Bobbe's frying pan, to eat swaddled in cool sour cream, the contrasting textures and temperatures indelibly printing themselves on our memory....

[After Moskowitz married and had children, the tradition continued.] Friends came each Chanukah and brought their children to celebrate with ours. We exchanged small gifts: boxes of crayons, pretty bars of soap, cellophane bags of sour candies for Grandma, who, of course, supplied the latkes. Early in the afternoon, she would begin grating potatoes on a vicious four-sided grater, the invention of some fiendish anti-Semite who must have seen the opportunity to maim half the Jewish population each December.

The trick was to finish grating just before the guests arrived so the potatoes would not blacken, as they have a discouraging tendency to do. Meanwhile, as she mixed in eggs, matzo meal, salt, and baking powder, Grandma heated a frying pan with enough oil to light the Chanukah lamps into the next century. The finished latkes were drained on supermarket paper bags that promptly turned translucent with fat. Still, we ate them: great, golden, greasy, dolloped-with-sour cream latkes, and our complaints became part of our Chanukah tradition, too....

But this year something is different; suddenly, finally, *I* am the grandma who makes the latkes. Two little grandchildren, both named for my mother-in-law (may she rest in peace), will come to our house to watch us light the menorah. Baby Helen at two and a half can already say the Hebrew blessing over the candles, and if my joy in that could translate to Chanukah gelt, all the banks in America would be forced to close.

I close my eyes and think of Grandma tasting a bit of her childhood each Chanukah when she prepared the latkes as her mother had made them before her. My mother, my aunts, my own grandmothers float back to me, young and vibrant once more, making days holy in the sanctuaries of their kitchens, feeding me, cradling me, connecting me to the intricately plaited braid of their past, and even at this moment, looking down the corridor of what's to come, I see myself join them as they open their arms wide to enfold my children and grandchildren in their embrace.

In today's United States, Jewish foods are enjoyed by many Americans. Maxwell Dane, a partner in the advertising agency Doyle, Dane, Bernbach, recalled the problem of promoting one of the firm's first clients, Levy's Jewish Rye Bread.

Most of the population of the New York area is non-Jewish. How do you get them to buy a rye bread bearing the name of Levy's Jewish Rye? So we felt from a marketing point of view we had to appeal to the rest of the population, and that led to the development of the campaign "I love Levy's." So it caught on. Our principal medium was subway station advertising, where we could get color and penetration for a relatively modest expenditure.

We faced it frontally. It would have been kind of stupid to try to duck it. The only way to duck it, we would call it Smith's or McPherson's Jewish Rye Bread. The campaign used different and obvious ethnic groups to say "You don't have to be Jewish to love Levy's real Jewish Rye Bread"—a Chinese waiter, an Italian woman, a black youngster, and an American Indian.

So much for rye bread and rolls. I knew that the bagel, which, along with matzo ball and chicken soup, as the quintessential Jewish food, had arrived when one day, while I was traveling with my wife to an interview in South Carolina, we passed a huge building with this sign prominently displayed: IT'S BAGEL TIME AT THE KITCHENS OF SARA LEE GREENVILLE.

And later on I knew the bagel had totally assimilated when Burger King announced the sale of "bacon, ham, or sausage on a bagel."

Since the 1920s, Conservative and Reform congregations have developed the Bat Mitzvah (daughter of the commandments) ceremony to celebrate a girl's 13th birthday. This girl in California prepares for the event by learning to read the Torah. She uses a silver pointer so that her finger will not mar the letters, which are always copied in ink.

At a Bar Mitzvah party in Long Island, New York, the honored young man and his grandfather dance to the traditional lively music of this festive occasion.

Ruth Schulson in front
of a portrait of her
great-great-great-
grandfather Harmon
Hendricks (1771–
1838). His father,
Uriah Hendricks, ar-
rived in the English
colonies in 1755.

Henry S. Hendricks
and Rosalie Nathan
Hendricks, Ruth
Schulson's parents.

THE SCHULSON FAMILY

Hyman and Ruth Hendricks Schulson live in an apartment on the Upper West Side of Manhattan. A few blocks away is the synagogue of Shearith Israel, the oldest Jewish congregation in the United States. Ruth Schulson's great-great-great-great grandfather, Uriah Hendricks, became a member of Shearith Israel in the 1760s. But she traces her family tree even farther back than that—to the Sephardic Jews who arrived in the 1600s. On the walls of the apartment are many paintings of her ancestors. But the latest generations are represented as well, by a number of color photographs of the Schulsons' children and grandchildren. We begin the interview with Ruth Schulson.

Q: We've interviewed many people for this project, but none whose family has been in the United States as long as yours has.

We go back to Lewis Moses Gomez, who arrived in the United States in 1696. Some of my relatives even claim that our family is descended from the original 23 Jews who landed in New Amsterdam. We're also descended from the Nathans, the Seixases—all of the old Sephardic Jewish families of New York are related in some way.

When I grew up going to Shearith Israel, I did not even know there was a distinction between Sephardic Jews and Ashkenazi Jews. I was brought up just Jewish, you know. That was my religion. We belonged to a Sephardic synagogue, and that was our tradition. Today, the old families are almost gone, except for me and some of my cousins. My sister lives in California.

My father, Henry S. Hendricks, was president of the congregation for almost 16 years, not consecutively, because he believed the office should rotate. He was very active there, active in Sephardic affairs, chairman of the board of Jewish Family Service. So I grew up with parents who were active in the community, and I adopted that in my own life.

Q. How have you been active in Shearith Israel?

I was president of the Sisterhood, five years, and I was president of the Parents' Council, and a member of the Shearith Israel League. I went through all this when my children were growing up, followed the cycle.

I also worked briefly for the American Sephardic Federation, the women's division. I was president of the women's division of the Central Sephardic Jewish Committee. And I was president of the women's division of the American Friends of the AIU, Alliance Universal Israelité, which sponsors schools in France and Israel. [Shearith Israel held a dinner-dance in her honor in 1992, recognizing her many contributions to the community and the congregation.]

Q: Tell us about your childhood.

I went to Horace Mann School, a nondenominational school here in New York City. My mother was a Girl Scout leader. We didn't do only Jewish things. We are Americans of Jewish faith. That's what my father always used to say. I graduated from Columbia University, with a degree in early childhood education. I taught at the Lighthouse [a school for vision-impaired children] and later worked at a child-care center. My own sight was never good, and I was told I could not pass the vision test for a regular public school teacher. I married my husband Hyman in 1950. He was born in Jerusalem, and came here when he was five, during World War I. So our children are actually descendants of a first-generation immigrant and of a ninth-generation immigrant. My husband is an Ashkenazi Jew. In that sense, I married out of the family.

Q: Are your children still active in Shearith Israel?

No. One son lives in Texas, another in Florida. My daughter and her husband live in Riverdale [an area of the Bronx in New York City]. The family has shrunk, like all families. People now live in different places. So why should I complain? My daughter lives in Riverdale. I call that next door. She and her husband have two young sons, and they all come back to Shearith Israel for the High Holidays.

My son-in-law carries the safer [a scroll that contains the text of the Torah]. In Shearith Israel on the High Holidays, the men dress in morning coats and high top hats. That became a tradition in the 19th century, when that was formal dress for men, and it continues today. We found my father's old top hat, but it doesn't fit anybody, so no one wears it now.

Q: Did you have Passover Seder here at home?

Up until this year I did. We always had it when I was a girl. All the family came, my aunt and uncle and cousins, great-aunt, and grandparents. Passover we always had chicken with apples. My mother didn't like cranberries. Chicken soup with matzo balls. Potatoes, not rice, because there's a question as to whether you should have rice on Passover. String beans, strawberries, and meal cake, which is a moist sort of sponge cake.

This year, my daughter Anne and her family went down to Florida to have Seder with my son's family. My son wanted me to make the family haroset and ship it to them. But Anne said, "Mom, I can do it," and she did—which I think in a way was better. She taught Jaimee and Loree, her daughters, how to make the harrada. The children have kept up the tradition. I have four granddaughters, three in Florida and one in Texas. Two of my three grandsons are here in New York. They observe all the holidays.

Frances Isaacs Hendricks, the wife of Harmon Hendricks, gave birth to 13 children. Below her portrait are photographs of the newest members of the Hendricks-Schulson family.

The Hendricks family Bible, printed in Spanish. The inscription on the left-hand page was written by Isaac Mattathias Gomez, who inherited it in 1788.

Hyman Schulson and Ruth Hendricks Schulson.

A map shows two plots of land in Manhattan owned by Frances Hendricks, a 19th-century ancestor of Ruth Schulson. In those days, the upper part of Manhattan was still farmland.

Q: How does Sephardic cooking differ from other types of Jewish cooking?

I tell everybody that I was brought up on Yankee cooking, because that's what it was. We had chicken soup, chicken, roast beef, pudding. The harosas that I make are said to be Moroccan, so the recipe must have come from some Spanish ancestors. Sephardic recipes are really Greek, Turkish, North African—wherever your ancestors came from. Joan Nathan, who recently wrote a book about Jewish cooking, borrowed from me a recipe for almond pudding. Originally it came from my Aunt Emily Nathan.

Hyman Schulson joins us at this point in the interview. He came to the United States from Palestine with his parents around 1918.

Q: Why did your parents decide to come here?

Because when my grandfather had come to this country earlier, he became a citizen. In so doing, he registered me, who was an infant then, and his family as citizens. My family had been settlers in what was then Palestine for over 300 years. But during World War I, the fighting reached that area, and people began to flee. My father came here, leaving my mother and me until he was able to take care of us. My mother and I came in on the S.S. *Chicago*. We went through Ellis Island. By virtue of my grandfather's citizenship, we were given preference.

My father was a rabbi. He obtained a job with a congregation in Bridgeport, Connecticut, where I went to high school, public school. After graduation, my father wanted me to go to yeshiva [a Jewish school to prepare students for the rabbinate], but I rebelled. I did attend a yeshiva for a short time, but I said, "Pop, this is not for me," and I enrolled in Brown University, where I had a scholarship. I was a member of Phi Beta Kappa and majored in philosophy.

I graduated from Brown in 1933 and the commencement speaker at my graduation was no less than Supreme Court Justice Benjamin N. Cardozo. He gave a famous speech called "Facts," which became a classic. Ruth's parents drove him up. They were cousins, but I had never met them, I had never met Ruth. They didn't know that their future son-in-law was present.

Ruth Schulson:

I was in high school then. My mother's father, Edgar Nathan, was a cousin of Cardozo's, and his law partner. I knew Cardozo when I was young. When I was about 14, we went to see him at his house in Westchester. As a child, I knew only that he worked in Washington.

Hyman Schulson:

Later I went to Yale Law School, where I also had a scholarship. After graduation, I took a job with the National Labor Relations Board [an agency of the U.S. government], as a lawyer in the review division. I was there from 1936 to 1939. I tried the Memorial Day riot case against Republic Steel at that time, and Inland Steel, which was the first sit-down strike case.

One day I was traveling from Chicago to Washington and I met Dr. Solomon Goldman, who was president of the Zionist Organization of America. We spent eight hours on the train. He asked me, "What are you doing?" I told him, and he said, "Don't take any other work. I have something for you in which you can be very useful and helpful." He had just come back from the World Zionist Congress, in which they discussed all the troubles that the Jews were having in Hitler's Germany. Dr. Goldman said, "We need a young man like you, who knows Hebrew, from a good Jewish background."

No sooner do I get back to my office in Washington than I get a call. That was the beginning of my work with the Zionist movement. We bought a building on 16th Street and organized a staff. I was put in charge of political work in Washington, and gave up my law practice for a while.

From 1942 to 1946, during World War II, I served in the U.S. Army Air Force. I also gave lectures to help sell U.S. Bonds. After the war, I continued with my work for a Jewish state. It led to the creation of the United Nations Special Committee on Palestine. In 1947, Israel filed an application to be admitted to the United Nations, and that led to the creation of the state of Israel in 1948.

Q: The following year, you met Ruth.

Her parents were not Zionists. They were nearer the other end. In Washington, I met David Wainhouse, a cousin of theirs, who introduced us. He was the best man at the wedding.

Ruth Schulson:

His wife was my father's first cousin. Actually, we met on a blind date.

Q. In your marriage, you have combined two very different Jewish traditions.

Hyman Schulson:

Yes, but I always maintain that ours is the oldest, because ours is from Palestine. These were Jews from America. I didn't fight with them. I argued with them, persuasively sometimes, otherwise not. That doesn't matter. I said to Ruth, what we make of it, the two of us, is what's important.

Ruth Schulson:

I remember my father always told me, "You have to be your own person and go forward on your own."

HENDRICKS-SCHULSON FAMILY ALMOND PUDDING

INGREDIENTS

4 eggs, separated
1/2 cup and 2 tbs. sugar
3/4 cup ground blanched almonds
1/2 tsp. almond extract (optional)
oil
matzoh meal
1 pt. strawberries or 1 cup strawberry puree

1. Beat the eggs till they are foamy. Add 1/2 cup sugar and beat until yolks are very pale and fluffy. Add almonds and extract, and mix till well blended.
2. In another bowl beat egg whites till stiff peaks form.
3. Fold egg whites into yolk mix and turn into an 8-inch soufflé dish that has been lightly coated with oil and then dusted with matzoh meal.
4. Bake in pre-heated 350 degree oven for 35 minutes or till golden. Let cool slightly.
5. Sprinkle top with the 2 tbs. of sugar. Top with fresh strawberries or strawberry puree. (Confectioner's sugar contains cornstarch and is thus prohibited at Passover.)

Hyman and Ruth Schulson with their children and grandchildren.

121

JEWISH AMERICAN TIMELINE

1654
A group of 23 Jews arrives in the Dutch colony of New Amsterdam.

1730
Congregation Shearith Israel builds the first American synagogue, in New York City.

1763
Dedication of Touro Synagogue in Newport, Rhode Island. It is today the oldest in the United States.

1778–1781
Haym Salomon helps to raise more than $650,000 to finance the American Revolution.

1826
Maryland is the last state to repeal laws barring Jews from public office.

1840–1880
Jewish American population rises from 15,000 to 300,000. Most new immigrants during this time were Ashkenazi Jews from central Europe.

1843
Founding of Independent Order of B'nai B'rith, first national Jewish fraternal organization.

1855
Immigrant landing station opens at Castle Garden in New York City.

1873
Founding of the Union of American Hebrew Congregations, composed of Reform Jewish leaders.

1880–1924
About 2.5 million Jewish immigrants arrive in the United States. Most were from eastern Europe, particularly Russia.

1881
Hebrew Immigrant Aid Society is founded to assist new immigrants in adjusting to American life.

1886
Samuel Gompers is elected first president of the American Federation of Labor.

1887
Jewish Theological Seminary of America is founded as a center of learning for the Conservative Jewish movement.

1888
United Hebrew Trades, the first nationwide organization of Jewish workers, is founded.

1892
Ellis Island becomes the major immigrant landing station.

1893
The Educational Alliance is founded to provide classes and recreation for Jewish immigrants. The National Council of Jewish Women is founded to provide services to immigrants.

1897
Jewish Daily Forward is founded, with Abraham Cahan as editor. It became the leading Yiddish-language newspaper in the United States.

1900
Workmen's Circle, an organization of Jewish laborers, is founded to help those who were unemployed or unable to work.

1907
Albert A. Michelson is the first American to receive a Nobel Prize. (He was awarded the prize for physics.)

1912
Henrietta Szold founds Hadassah, which became the Women's Zionist Organization of America.

1913
B'nai B'rith establishes the Anti-Defamation League to fight bigotry against all ethnic and racial groups.

1915
Leo Frank is lynched in Georgia.

1916
Louis D. Brandeis becomes the first Jewish Supreme Court justice.

1939
The United Jewish Appeal is organized to raise funds to provide support for European Jewish refugees. After World War II, it continued its activities on behalf of Jewish settlers in Israel.

1945–52
About 140,000 Jewish refugees from Europe arrive in the United States.

1958
Leonard Bernstein becomes the first American-born conductor of the New York Philharmonic orchestra.

1978
Isaac Bashevis Singer is awarded the Nobel Prize for literature. He is the only Yiddish-language author ever to receive the prize.

1994
Steven Spielberg wins the Academy Award for best director for *Schindler's List,* a film about the Holocaust.

FURTHER READING

General Accounts of Jewish American History

Fishman, Priscilla. *The Jews of the United States*. New York: Quadrangle, 1973.

Hertzberg, Arthur. *The Jews in America*. New York: Simon & Schuster, 1989.

Howe, Irving. *World of Our Fathers*. New York: Harcourt, Brace, 1976.

Karp, Abraham J. *Golden Door to America: The Jewish Immigrant Experience*. New York: Penguin, 1976.

———. *Haven and Home: A History of the Jews in America*. New York: Schocken, 1985.

Levitan, Tina. *Jews in American Life from 1492 to the Space Age*. New York: Hebrew Publishing, 1969.

Rochlin, Harriet, and Fred Rochlin. *Pioneer Jews: A New Life in the Far West*. Boston: Houghton Mifflin, 1984.

Sachar, Howard M. *A History of the Jews in America*. New York: Knopf, 1992.

Sanders, Ronald. *Shores of Refuge: A Hundred Years of Jewish Emigration*. New York: Schocken, 1988.

Schappes, Morris U., ed. *A Documentary History of the Jews in the United States, 1654–1875*. New York: Schocken, 1971.

Schappes, Morris U. *The Jews in the United States*. New York: Tercentenary Book Committee, 1958.

Weinberg, Sydney Stahl. *The World of Our Mothers*. Chapel Hill: University of North Carolina Press, 1988.

Personal Accounts of Jewish American Life

Angel, Marc D. *Sephardic Voices, 1492–1992*. New York: Hadassah, 1991.

Benny, Jack, and Joan Benny. *Sunday Nights at Seven: The Jack Benny Story*. New York: Warner, 1990.

Chyet, Stanley F., ed. *Lives and Voices*. Philadelphia: The Jewish Publication Society of America, 5732/1972.

Goldman, Emma. *Living My Life*. 1931. Reprint. New York: Dover, 1970.

Howe, Irving, and Kenneth Libo, eds. *How We Lived: A Documentary History of Immigrant Jews in America, 1880–1930*. New York: Richard Marek, 1979.

Jastrow, Marie. *Looking Back: The American Dream through Immigrant Eyes, 1907–1918*. New York: Norton, 1986.

Kramer, Sydelle, and Jenny Masur, eds. *Jewish Grandmothers*. Boston: Beacon Press, 1976.

Libo, Kenneth, and Irving Howe, eds. *We Lived There Too: Pioneer Jews and the Westward Movement of America* New York: St. Martin's/Marek, 1984.

Marcus, Jacob Rader. *Memoirs of American Jews, 1775–1865*. Philadelphia: Jewish Publication Society of America, 5715/1955.

Meltzer, Milton. *The Jewish Americans: A History in Their Own Words, 1650–1950*. New York: Crowell, 1982.

Moskowitz, Faye. *And the Bridge Is Love*. Boston: Beacon Press, 1991.

Ribalow, Harold U., comp. *Autobiographies of American Jews*. Philadelphia: Jewish Publication Society of America, 5733/1973.

Rubin, Steven J., ed. *Writing Our Lives: Autobiographies of American Jews*. Philadelphia: Jewish Publication Society, 5751/1991.

Simon, Kate. *Bronx Primitive: Portraits in a Childhood*. New York: Viking, 1982.

Simons, Howard. *Jewish Times: Voices of the American Jewish Experience*. Boston: Houghton Mifflin, 1988.

Novels and Stories of Jewish American Life

Bellow, Saul. *Herzog*. New York: Viking, 1964.

Gold, Herbert. *Fathers*. New York: Random House, 1966.

Malamud, Bernard. *A New Life*. New York: Farrar Straus & Giroux, 1961.

Potok, Chaim. *The Chosen*. New York: Simon & Schuster, 1967.

Rosten, Leo. *The Education of H*Y*M*A*N K*A*P*L*A*N*. New York: Harper & Row, 1959.

Roth, Henry. *Call It Sleep*. 1934. Reprint. New York: Noonday Press, 1961.

Roth, Philip. *Goodbye, Columbus*. New York: Vintage, 1993.

Salinger, J. D. *Franny and Zooey*. Boston: Little, Brown, 1961.

Wouk, Herman. *City Boy*. 1952. Reprint. Boston: Back Bay Books, 1992.

Wallant, Edward Lewis. *The Pawnbroker*. New York: Harcourt Brace Jovanovich, 1978.

Yezierska, Anzia. *Breadgivers*. 1925. Reprint. New York: Persea Books, 1975.

TEXT CREDITS

Main Text

p. 15, top: Ellen Umansky and Dianne Ashton, eds., *Four Centuries of Jewish Women's Spirituality* (Boston: Beacon Press, 1992), 82-83.

p. 15, bottom: Josephine Goldmark, *Pilgrims of '48* (New Haven: Yale University Press, 1930), 185.

p. 16, top: Hamilton Holt, ed., *The Life Stories of Undistinguished Americans as Told by Themselves* (New York: Routledge, 1990), 21-22.

p. 16, bottom: Irving Howe and Kenneth Libo, eds., *How We Lived: A Documentary History of Immigrant Jews in America, 1880–1930* (New York: Richard Marek, 1979), 5.

p. 17, top: Stanley F. Chyet, ed., *Lives and Voices* (Philadelphia: The Jewish Publication Society of America, 5732/ 1972), 115-116.

p. 17, bottom: Reprinted from *American Mosaic: The Immigrant Experience in the Words of Those Who Lived It,* by Joan Morrison and Charlotte Fox Zabusky, by permission of the University of Pittsburgh Press. © 1980, 1993 by Joan Morrison and Charlotte Fox Zabusky, 8-9.

p. 18, top: Milton Meltzer, *The Jewish Americans: A History in Their Own Words, 1650–1950* (New York: Crowell, 1982), 64-65.

p. 18, bottom: Howe and Libo, *How We Lived,* 9-10.

p. 19, top: Ronald Takaki, *A Different Mirror: A History of Multicultural America* (Boston: Little, Brown, 1993), 278.

p. 19, bottom: Elizabeth Hasanovitz, *One of Them* (Boston: Houghton Mifflin, 1918), 6-7.

p. 20, top: Abraham J. Peck, ed., *The German-Jewish Legacy in America, 1938–1988* (Detroit: Wayne State University Press, 1989), 51-54.

p. 20, bottom: Peck, *The German-Jewish Legacy,* 81-83.

p. 21: Reprinted from *American Mosaic: The Immigrant Experience in the Words of Those Who Lived It,* by Joan Morrison and Charlotte Fox Zabusky, by permission of the University of Pittsburgh Press. © 1980, 1993 by Joan Morrison and Charlotte Fox Zabusky, 155-157.

p. 22: Giles R. Wright, ed., *Looking Back: Eleven Life Histories* (Trenton: New Jersey Historical Commission, 1986), 50-54.

p. 26: Jacob Rader Marcus, *Memoirs of American Jews, 1775–1865,* vol. 3 (Philadelphia: Jewish Publication Society, 5715/1955), 24-25.

p. 27, top: Umansky and Ashton, *Four Centuries of Jewish Women's Spirituality,* 94-95.

p. 27, bottom: Chyet, *Lives and Voices,* 242-44.

p. 28, top: Abraham J. Karp, *Golden Door to America: The Jewish Immigrant Experience* (New York: Penguin, 1976), 72-73.

p. 28, bottom: Katharine Emsden, ed., *Coming to America: A New Life in a New Land* (Lowell, Mass.: Discovery Enterprises, 1993), 19-22.

p. 29, top: Howe and Libo, *How We Lived,* 20-21.

p. 29, bottom: From Ellis Island Museum transcript of Celia Adler interview. Courtesy of National Park Service.

p. 30, top: Howard M. Sachar, *A History of the Jews in America* (New York: Knopf, 1992), 120.

p. 30, bottom: Louis Waldman, *Labor Lawyer* (New York: Dutton, 1944), 19-20.

p. 31, top: Giles R. Wright, ed., *The Journey from Home* (Trenton: New Jersey Historical Commission, 1986), 21.

p. 31, bottom: Wright, *The Journey from Home,* 22.

p. 32: Sachar, *A History of the Jews in America,* 41.

p. 33, top: Waldman, *Labor Lawyer,* 20.

p. 33, middle: Meltzer, *The Jewish Americans,* 70-71.

p. 33, bottom: Peck, *The German-Jewish Legacy,* 111.

p. 38, top: Kenneth Libo and Irving Howe, eds., *We Lived There Too: Pioneer Jews and the Westward Movement of America* (New York: St. Martin's/Marek, 1984), 46.

p. 38, bottom: Libo and Howe, *We Lived There Too,* 51-52.

p. 39: Karp, *Golden Door to America,* 25-27.

p. 40, top: Marcus, *Memoirs of American Jews,* vol. 1, 346.

p. 40, middle: Emma Goldman, *Living My Life* (New York: Dover, 1970), 11-12.

p. 40, bottom: Chyet, *Lives and Voices,* 245-248.

p. 41, top: Steven Lowenstein, *The Jews of Oregon* (Portland: Jewish Historical Society of Oregon, 1987), 74.

p. 41, middle: Wright, *The Journey from Home,* 35.

p. 41, bottom: From Ellis Island Museum transcript of Fannie Shamits Friedman interview. Courtesy of National Park Service.

p. 42, top: From Ellis Island Museum transcript of Celia Adler interview. Courtesy of National Park Service.

p. 42, bottom: Wright, *The Journey from Home,* 34.

p. 43, top: Wright, *The Journey from Home,* 12.

p. 43, bottom: June Namias, *First Generation* (Boston: Beacon Press, 1975), 125-26.

p. 44, top: Goldmark, *Pilgrims of '48,* 289.

p. 44, middle: Goldmark, *Pilgrims of '48,* 250-51.

p. 44, bottom: Marcus, *Memoirs of American Jews,* vol. 3, 26-27.

p. 45: Harold U. Ribalow, comp., *Autobiographies of American Jews* (Philadelphia: Jewish Publication Society of America, 5733/1973), 55-56.

p. 46, top: Reprinted from *American Mosaic: The Immigrant Experience in the Words of Those Who Lived It,* by Joan Morrison and Charlotte Fox Zabusky, by permission of the University of Pittsburgh Press. © 1980, 1993 by Joan Morrison and Charlotte Fox Zabusky, 1.

p. 46, bottom: Waldman, *Labor Lawyer,* 20-21.

p. 47, top: Elizabeth Ewen, *Immigrant Women in the Land of Dollars* (New York: Monthly Review Press, 1985), 68.

p. 47, bottom: Eric H. Cornell, *The Lord Is My Shepherd,* unpublished manuscript, 30-31.

p. 52, top: Karp, *Golden Door to America,* 50-51.

p. 52, bottom: Karp, *Golden Door to America,* 55-57.

p. 53, top: Marcus, *Memoirs of American Jews,* vol. 1, 356.

p. 53, bottom: Libo and Howe, *We Lived There Too,* 137-138.

p. 54: Louis Wolens interview, Navarro College Oral History Collection, November 1977.

p. 55, top: Waldman, *Labor Lawyer,* 22-23.

p. 55, bottom: Ribalow, *Autobiographies of American Jews,* 63-64.

p. 56, top: Eleanor F. Horvitz, "Pushcarts, Surreys With Fringe on Top: The Story of the Jews of the North End," *Rhode Island Jewish Historical Notes* 8, no. 1 (November 1979): 17.

p. 56, bottom: Karp, *Golden Door to America,* 170-71.

p. 57: Ribalow, *Autobiographies of American Jews,* 171-73.

p. 58: Reprinted from *American Mosaic: The Immigrant Experience in the Words of Those Who Lived It,* by Joan Morrison and Charlotte Fox Zabusky, by permission of the University of Pittsburgh Press. © 1980, 1993 by Joan Morrison and Charlotte Fox Zabusky, 9-11.

p. 59: Howe and Libo, *How We Lived,* 136.

p. 60, top: Goldman, *Living My Life,* 16.

p. 60, bottom: Meltzer, *The Jewish Americans,* 77-79.

p. 61: Waldman, *Labor Lawyer,* 30-31.

p. 62: Meltzer, *The Jewish Americans,* 109-112.

p. 63, top: Holt, *Life Stories,* 28.

p. 63, bottom: Howe and Libo, *How We Lived,* 141-43.

p. 64: Howe and Libo, *How We Lived,* 177.

p. 65: Waldman, *Labor Lawyer,* 37-38.

p. 66: Libo and Howe, *We Lived There Too,* 154-55.

p. 67: Meltzer, *The Jewish Americans,* 37-39.

p. 68, top: Marcus, *Memoirs of American Jews,* vol. 2, 264-66.

p. 68, bottom: Morris U. Schappes, ed., *A Documentary History of the Jews in the United States* (New York: Schocken, 1971), 367.

p. 69, top: Floyd S. Fierman, *Guts and Ruts: The Jewish Pioneer on the Trail in the American Southwest* (Hoboken, N.J.: Ktav, 1985), 116.

p. 69, bottom: Libo and Howe, *We Lived There Too,* 286.

p. 70, top: Leonard Dinnerstein, *Anti-Semitism in America* (New York: Oxford University Press, 1994), 41.

p. 70, middle: Horvitz, "Pushcarts, Surreys With Fringe on Top," 25.

p. 70, bottom: Libo and Howe, *We Lived There Too,* 238-39.

p. 72, top: Emsden, *Coming to America,* 54-55.

p. 72, bottom: Clifford M. Kuhn, Joye Harlowe, and Bernard West, *Living Atlanta: An Oral History of the City, 1914–1948* (Athens: University of Georgia Press, 1990), 254.

p. 73: Howard Simons, *Jewish Times* (New York: Anchor, 1990), 78-79.

p. 78, top: Meltzer, *The Jewish Americans,* 43-45.

p. 78, bottom: Marcus, *Memoirs of American Jews,* vol. 3, 57-58.

p. 79: Samuel Chotzinoff, *A Lost Paradise* (New York: Knopf, 1955), 70-71.

p. 80, top: Lowenstein, *The Jews of Oregon,* 93-94.

p. 80, bottom: Howe and Libo, *How We Lived,* 54.

p. 81, top: Giles R. Wright, ed., *Arrival and Settlement in a New Place* (Trenton: New Jersey Historical Commission, 1986), 11.

p. 81, bottom: Marie Jastrow, *Looking Back: The American Dream Through Immigrant Eyes, 1907–1918* (New York: Norton, 1986), 39.

p. 82: Holt, *Life Stories,* 26-28.

p. 83, top: Theodore White, *In Search of History: A Personal Adventure* (New York: Harper & Row, 1978), 26-27.

p. 83, bottom: Simons, *Jewish Times,* 75-76.

p. 84, top: Chotzinoff, *A Lost Paradise,* 101-2.

p. 84, bottom: Oral history of Sara J. Abrams (New York: YIVO Institute for Jewish Studies, box 9, folder 92.

p. 85: Howe and Libo, *How We Lived,* 274.

p. 86: Marcus, *Memoirs of American Jews,* vol. 3, 56-57, 59.

p. 87: Libo and Howe, *We Lived There Too,* 227, 230.

p. 88, top: Martin Levin, ed., *Five Boyhoods* (Garden City, N.Y.: Doubleday, 1962), 37.

p. 88, bottom: Howe and Libo, *How We Lived,* 126-27.

p. 89, top: Meltzer, *The Jewish Americans,* 107-9.

p. 89, bottom: Sachar, *A History of the Jews in America,* 148.

p. 90, top: Howe and Libo, *How We Lived,* 88.

p. 90, bottom: White, *In Search of History,* 19.

p. 91, top: Steven J. Rubin, ed., *Writing Our Lives: Autobiographies of American Jews* (Philadelphia: The Jewish Publication Society of America, 5751/ 1991), 333-34.

p. 91, bottom: Peck, *The German-Jewish Legacy,* 184-85.

p. 92: Meltzer, *The Jewish Americans,* 53-56.

p. 93: Howe and Libo, *How We Lived,* 122.

p. 94: Chyet, *Lives and Voices,* 134-36.

p. 95: Faye Moskowitz, *And The Bridge Is Love* (Boston: Beacon Press, 1991), 41-44.

p. 96: Simons, *Jewish Times,* 230-31.

p. 97: Jacob J. Javits, with Rafael Steinberg, *Javits: The Autobiography of a Public Man* (Boston: Houghton Mifflin, 1981), 7-8.

p. 98: Jastrow, *Looking Back,* 97-99.

p. 99: Chotzinoff, *A Lost Paradise,* 63-64, 76-78.

p. 100: Kuhn, Harlowe, and West, *Living Atlanta,* 256-57.

p. 101: Giles R. Wright, Howard L. Green, and Lee R. Parks, eds., *Schooling and Education* (Trenton: New Jersey Historical Commission, 1987), 22.

p. 102, top: Howe and Libo, *How We Lived,* 73-74.

p. 102, bottom: Ribalow, *Autobiographies of American Jews,* 353-54.

p. 103: Eli N. Evans, *The Provincials: A Personal History of Jews in the South* (New York: Atheneum, 1973), 113.

p. 108, top: Ann Banks, *First-Person America* (New York: Knopf, 1980), 208.

p. 108, bottom: Howe and Libo, *How We Lived,* 70.

p. 109: Henny Youngman, with Neal Karlen, *Take My Life, Please* (New York: William Morrow, 1991), 108-112.

p. 110, top: Abe Burrows, *Honest, Abe, Is There Really No Business Like Show Business?* (Boston: Atlantic Monthly Press, 1980), 291-92.

p. 110, bottom: Jack Benny and Joan Benny, *Sunday Nights at Seven: The Jack Benny Story* (New York: Warner, 1990), 6-11.

p. 112: Wright, *Looking Back,* 54.

p. 113, top: Jerome R. Mintz, *Hasidic People: A Place in the New World* (Cambridge: Harvard University Press, 1992), 4.

p. 113, middle: Giles R. Wright, ed., *The Reasons for Migrating* (Trenton: New Jersey Historical Commission, 1986), 29.

p. 113, bottom: Mary Motley Kalergis, *Home of the Brave* (New York: Dutton, 1989), unpaged.

p. 114: Rubin, *Writing Our Lives,* 78-79.

p. 115: Umansky and Ashton, *Four Centuries,* 204.

p. 116: Moskowitz, *And the Bridge Is Love,* 20-26.

p. 117: Simons, *Jewish Times,* 312.

Sidebars

p. 16: Jacob Rader Marcus, *Memoirs of American Jews, 1775–1865,* vol. 2 (Philadelphia: Jewish Publication Society of America: 5715/1955), 290.

p. 23: Ronald Takaki, *A Different Mirror* (Boston: Little Brown, 1993), 376-77.

p. 28: Abraham J. Karp, *Golden Door to America* (New York: Penguin, 1976), 41.

p. 31: Giles R. Wright, *The Reasons for Migrating* (Trenton: New Jersey Historical Commission, 1986), 24.

p. 33: Reprinted from *American Mosaic: The Immigrant Experience in the Words of Those Who Lived It,* by Joan Morrison and Charlotte Fox Zabusky, by permission of the University of Pittsburgh Press. © 1980, 1993 by Joan Morrison and Charlotte Fox Zabusky, 9.

p. 47: Personal interview with Sydney Schwartz.

p. 55: Irving Howe and Kenneth Libo, eds., *How We Lived: A Documentary History of Immigrant Jews in America, 1880–1930* (New York: Richard Marek, 1979), 70.

p. 60: Hamilton Holt, ed., *The Life Stories of Undistinguished Americans as Told by Themselves* (New York: Routledge, 1990), 22.

p. 63: Herbert Gutman, et al., *Who Built America?* (New York: Pantheon, 1992), 190.

p. 67: Howard M. Sachar, *A History of the Jews in America* (New York: Knopf, 1992), 56.

p. 73: Sachar, *A History of the Jews in America,* 280.

p. 83: Takaki, *A Different Mirror,* 284.

p. 85: Sachar, *A History of the Jews in America,* 210.

p. 89: Takaki, *A Different Mirror,* 287.

p. 92: Giles R. Wright, Howard L. Green, and Lee R. Parks, eds., *Schooling and Education* (Trenton: New Jersey Historical Commission, 1987), 32.

p. 101: Howard L. Green and Lee R. Parks, *What Is Ethnicity?* (Trenton: New Jersey Historical Commission, 1987), 14.

p. 116: Steven Lowenstein, *The Jews of Oregon* (Portland: Jewish Historical Society of Oregon, 1987), 87.

p. 121: Adapted from Joan Nathan, *Jewish Cooking in America* (New York: Knopf, 1994), 330.

Amalgamated Clothing and Textile Workers: 63, 82 bottom; American Jewish Archives: 39, 43, 65, 66 bottom, 114 top; courtesy of the American Jewish Historical Society, Waltham, Mass.: 30, 38 bottom, 51, 53 top, 69 top, 84 top, 85, 97 top, 100; Anti-Defamation League of B'nai B'rith: 70, 71, 72, 73; Arizona Historical Society Library: 48 (#46490); Courtesy of the Leo Baeck Institute, New York: 10, 13, 16, 17 top and bottom, 20 bottom, 21 bottom, 29; Balch Institute for Ethnic Studies Library: 45 top, 87 bottom (Albert Einstein Medical Center photo collection), 96 bottom (Joseph Paul photo collection); courtesy Ira M. Beck Memorial Archives of Rocky Mountain Jewish History, University of Denver: 68 top; Aron and Manette Berlinger: 19 bottom, 20 top; Elisheva Berlinger: 104; Fanny Berlinger: 15 top; Bluthenthal family collection: cover photo, 94 bottom; by permission of the British Library, *Lisbon Mishneh Torah,* Harley MS 5698 f434v: cover background; Brown Brothers: 64 top; Central Armed Forces Museum, Moscow, courtesy of the United States Holocaust Memorial Museum: 22 top; Chicago Historical Society: 62 bottom (ICHi-21014), 78 bottom (DN 68,697), 80 top (CRC-144-I); Chicago Jewish Archives/Spertus Institute: 18 bottom; Cincinnati Historical Society, Ransohoff Collection: 116; J. Kirk Condyles, Impact Visuals: 117 bottom; courtesy Congregation Shearith Israel, New York: 38 top and middle; Culver Pictures: 62 top; George Eastman House: 59 bottom, 60, 61 bottom; Ellis Island Immigration Museum: 37 (Augustus Sherman Collection), 41 bottom, 44; Robert Fox, Impact Visuals: 113; Franklin D. Roosevelt Library: 22 bottom; Hadassah, New York City: 103; Historical Association of Southern Florida: 96 top; Idaho State Historical Society: 86 bottom (#73-20.13); Immigrant City Archives: 8; Institute of Texan Cultures, San Antonio: 5 (*San Antonio Light* collection), 40 bottom (Archives of Temple B'nai Israel, Galveston), 42 top, 56 top, 91 top (courtesy of Mr. & Mrs. L. H. Golden), 102 bottom, 112 top (courtesy United HIAS Service); Jewish Archives of the Historical Society of Western Pennsylvania, Pittsburgh: 53 bottom (Roth family photographs), 87 top (Paradise/Goodman family photographs), 89 (Nobel/ Gartner family photographs), 93 (Roth family photographs); Archives of the Jewish Federation of Nashville and Middle Tennessee: 79 top; Jewish Historical Society of Maryland, Inc.: 32 top and bottom, 81 bottom; Jewish Historical Society of Oregon: 67, 74, 94 top; Evan Johnson, Impact Visuals: 117 top; Lauterwasser, courtesy Unitel: 110; Lewis W. Hine Collection, U.S. History, Local History and Genealogy Division, the New York Public Library, Astor, Lenox and Tilden Foundations: 41 top, 61 top; Library of Congress: 24, 34, 58 bottom, 78 top, 82 top, 91 bottom; courtesy of Milwaukee County Historical Society: 12, 90 top, 114 bottom, 115 (Erwin Gebhard, *Milwaukee Sentinel*); the Montana Historical Society, Helena: 68 bottom; Museum of the City of New York: 84 bottom (Byron collection), 92 (Jacob Riis collection), 98 top (Jacob Riis collection), 99 top (Jacob Riis collection), 101 (Jacob Riis collection); National Archives: 28 bottom, 42 bottom, 77; National Archives, Washington, D.C., courtesy of the United States Holocaust Memorial Museum, 23; National Museum of American Jewish History, Philadelphia: 83, 107; Nebraska State Historical Society: 66 top; 69 bottom (Solomon D. Butcher collection); courtesy the *New York Times:* 57; Ohlinger: 108 top and bottom, 109, 111 top and bottom; Oregon Historical Society: 80 bottom (#86411), 95 (#25946); courtesy of Mandy Patinkin: 6-7; Peale Museum, Baltimore, Md.: 36, 40 top; Joseph J. Pennell Collection, Kansas Collection, University of Kansas Libraries: 76; Rhode Island Jewish Historical Association: frontispiece, 54 top, 56 bottom, 99 bottom; Linda Rosier, Impact Visuals: 112 bottom; courtesy of the Schulson family: 118-121; Security Pacific National Bank Photograph Collection/Los Angeles Public Library: 97 bottom, 106; Shashinka Photo Library: 21 top; Staten Island Historical Society: 52 top, 79 bottom, 81 top; Photography Collections, University of Maryland, Baltimore County: 52 bottom, 58 top, 59 top; Temple Beth El, courtesy of Rhode Island Jewish Historical Association: 86 top; Special Collections and Preservation Division, University of Washington Libraries, Seattle: 15 bottom (#UW 1006), 45 bottom (#UW 7530), 54 bottom (#UW 1092), 55 (#UW 1749); UPI/Bettmann: 33; Weidenfeld & Nicholson: 46; Western Jewish History Center: 90 bottom; Workmen's Circle/Arbeter Ring: 64 bottom; from the Archives of the YIVO Institute for Jewish Research: 11, 14, 18 top, 19 top, 26 top and bottom, 27 top and bottom, 28 top, 50, 102 top.

INDEX

ACKNOWLEDGMENTS

We want to thank Aron and Manette Berlinger, dear friends with whom we have shared many holidays as we watched their daughters and ours grow up together. Their own family album has contributed greatly to this book. We also owe thanks to Nancy Toff, executive editor of Oxford Children's and Young Adult Books, and to Ruth Bluthenthal Toff. Nancy's enthusiasm for the *American Family Albums* and her ideas for this particular book are responsible for any success it may have. We are proud to have her ancestors on the cover.

We must also acknowledge the generous help we received from Dr. Jeanne Abrams of the Rocky Mountain Jewish Historical Society; Linda Bailey of the Cincinnati Historical Society; Tom Beck of the University of Maryland, Baltimore County; Kathleen Brennan of the National Child Labor Committee; Diane Bruce of the Institute of Texan Cultures, San Antonio; Barbara J. Bush of the Arizona Historical Society; Carolyn Cole of the Los Angeles Public Library; Tara Deal, our patient and talented editor at Oxford University Press; Carlotta DeFillo of the Staten Island Historical Society; Stephen Frank and Abbey Krain of the National Museum of American Jewish History, Philadelphia; Patricia Friedland of the Community Service Society; Morris Gerber; Robert Goldberg; Debbie Goodsite and Sarah Partridge of the Bettmann Archive; Dawn Haas of the Milwaukee Journal-Sentinel Corporation; Lee Haas of the Jewish Federation of Nashville; Eleanor F. Horvitz of the Rhode Island Jewish Historical Association; Gina Hsin of the American Jewish Historical Society; Dawn Hugh of the Historical Museum of Southern Florida; Elizabeth P. Jacox of the Idaho State Historical Society; Kathy Lafferty of the University of Kansas Libraries; Marguerite Lavin and Tony Pisani of the Museum of the City of New York; Janice Madhu of the International Museum of Photography; Mary Markey of the City Life Museum Complex, Baltimore; Genya Markon and Denine Taylor of the U.S. Holocaust Memorial Museum; Diane H. Merlin of Workmen's Circle/Arbeter Ring; Laura Meyer of the Jewish Historical Society of Oregon; Gail Moss of the New York Public Library; Virginia North of the Jewish Historical Society of Maryland; Laura O'Hara of the Western Jewish History Center; Jane R. Ornauer of the Anti-Defamation League; Judith B. Ross of the Jewish Archives of the Historical Society of Western Pennsylvania; Rhonda Migdal Schwartz of Oxford University Press; Susan Seyl of the Oregon Historical Society; Eve Sicular and Nancy Abramson of the YIVO Institute for Jewish Research; Paul Sigrist and Barry Moreno of the Ellis Island Immigration Museum; Judith A. Simonsen of the Milwaukee County Historical Society; Ken Skulski of the Immigrant City Archives, Lawrence, Mass.; Dr. Diane Spielmann and Leo Greenbaum of the Leo Baeck Institute; Kathy Spray and Kevin Proffitt of the American Jewish Archives, Cincinnati; Norma Spungen of the Chicago Jewish Archives; Barbara Tritell of the Jewish Museum; Martha Vestecka-Miller of the Nebraska State Historical Society; Jack Womack of the Amalgamated Clothing and Textile Workers Union; and Linda Ziemer of the Chicago Historical Society.

We owe special thanks to Hyman Schulson and Ruth Hendricks Schulson for welcoming us into their home and sharing their memories with us. *L'chaim!*

ABOUT THE AUTHORS

Dorothy and Thomas Hoobler have published more than 50 books for children and young adults, including *Margaret Mead: A Life in Science; Vietnam: Why We Fought; Showa: The Age of Hirohito;* and *Photographing History: The Career of Mathew Brady.* Their works have been honored by the Society for School Librarians International, the Library of Congress, the New York Public Library, the National Council for Social Studies, and *Best Books for Children,* among other organizations and publications. The Hooblers have also written several volumes of historical fiction for children, including *Next Stop Freedom, Frontier Diary, The Summer of Dreams,* and *Treasure in the Stream.* Dorothy Hoobler received her master's degree in American history from New York University and worked as a textbook editor before becoming a full-time freelance editor and writer. Thomas Hoobler received his master's degree in education from Xavier University, and he previously worked as a teacher and textbook editor.